# The *Potluck* Club
# Cookbook

# The *Potluck* Club
# Cookbook

*Easy Recipes to Enjoy with Family and Friends*

## Linda Evans Shepherd
## and Eva Marie Everson

Revell

*a division of Baker Publishing Group*
Grand Rapids, Michigan

Published by Revell
a division of Baker Publishing Group
P.O. Box 6287, Grand Rapids, MI 49516-6287
www.revellbooks.com

Printed in the United States of America

Library of Congress Cataloging-in-Publication Data
Shepherd, Linda  E., 1957–
    The Potluck Club cookbook : easy recipes to enjoy with family and friends / Linda Evans Shepherd and Eva Marie Everson.
        p.   cm.
    Includes bibliographical references.
    ISBN 978-0-8007-3349-0 (pbk.)
    1. Cookery, American. I. Everson, Eva Marie. II. Shepherd, Linda E., 1957– Potluck Club. III. Title.
TX715.S14735  2009
641.5973—dc22                                              2009012205

**The Recipe for Friendship**

2 heaping cups of patience
2 handfuls of generosity
1 heart of love
A dash of laughter
2 well-rounded scoops of respect
2 heaping measures of trust
1 head of understanding
Sprinkle generously with kindness
Add plenty of faith and mix well

Spread over a lifetime and serve everyone you meet.

To my mom, who taught me everything I know about good recipes. I'm so glad you love this book. Thanks for making sure I got all our favorite recipes in tip-top shape—Linda

To Jessica, who takes the love of cooking from past generations to a whole new level—your mother, Eva

# Contents

**Potluck's Just Desserts—Desserts**

**Potluck Munches Brunch—Breakfast**

**Potluck Meets Meats—Meat Dishes**

**Potluck Veggies Out—Vegetables**

# Preface

I (Linda) recently met a woman who'd never been to a potluck. "What's it all about?" she wanted to know.

As a longtime potluck connoisseur, I explained it was about creating and bringing a dish to a party, dinner, brunch, dessert, or luncheon. "All of the guests create and share a dish. That way no one has the burden of making the entire meal themselves."

But there's more. Potlucks are about the fun of tasting a variety of culinary delights. It's about feeling loved as you indulge in dishes from your family and friends. Plus, potlucks provide an opportunity to share a meal with a group of people without killing yourself in the kitchen or running up your credit card bill in a restaurant. Dining together without the normal dinner-party headaches helps you concentrate on the reason you wanted to get together in the first place: connection, food, and fun.

If you've ever been lucky enough to walk a potluck buffet line, you've probably eaten a few helpings of gooey chocolate éclair dessert and helped yourself to a serving or two of someone's homemade cake. This means you'll appreciate the origin of the word *potluck*. It's from an English word formed from two words meaning "cooking pot" and "lucke," referring to anyone lucky enough to find food in a pot.

We have been lucky enough to attend many a potluck, and we've enjoyed them so much that we've written half a dozen or so novels about a group of ladies who love eating with friends as much as we do. Our first series, the Potluck Club, was followed by a second helping of our saucy characters and their recipes for both dishes and disaster in the Potluck Catering Club series.

If you are looking for opportunities to enjoy a potluck, consider hosting a:

- **Book Club Potluck**—Grab the latest Potluck novel and host a girls' night out with a dish to share from the pages of the novels. You can also give this recipe book as a gift to all your friends, then host a potluck dinner with a menu from this recipe collection. What yummy fun!

- **Snack Potluck**—Great for almost any social occasion like sporting events or craft get-togethers. Invite everyone to bring party snacks to share, like Eva's sausage-stuffed mushrooms or my caramel Ritz Bits crackers. You can't go wrong with Mom's cereal snacks, which Linda's mom spent forty years perfecting.

- **Chocolate Potluck**—Our favorite! Invite everyone to bring homemade chocolate desserts to sample. For ideas, check out recipes like Laura's microwave mint fudge or Eva's chocolate cream pie.

- **Potluck Lunch or Supper**—We've sampled these kinds of potlucks at church, in the neighborhood, and at the office. If you need an idea about what to bring to your next potluck, try whipping up Linda's pecan crusted baked chicken or Eva's chicken potpie. Use paper plates for a quick cleanup so you can concentrate on the fun and yum.

- **Salad Potluck**—Bring ingredients to create one big salad or bring a variety of salads to sample like Eva's mango salad or Linda's all-time favorite, layer salad with a secret ingredient.

- **Dessert Potluck**—Have the group bring desserts to share for your next after-dinner get-together. Try Eva's lemon meringue pie or Linda's cool and smooth four layer delight. It's an easy fix.

- **Ice Cream Potluck**—Why not try a giant banana split party with a variety of ice creams, toppings, and fruit. This is great fun for the kids.

- **Brunch Potluck**—Need to host an early morning get-together? Have your friends bring breakfast items or ingredients to create an oatmeal bar. You can also try our great breakfast recipes like

Eva's french toast soufflé or Linda's quick breakfast casserole, which you can prepare the night before.

- **Stew Potluck**—Each guest has an assignment to bring one item for the soon-to-be pot of bubbling stew. See our potluck vegetable beef stew recipe for complete directions on what to ask your guests to bring. You might also assign Mom's cornbread casserole to complete the experience. But then, it might take Eva's Georgia pumpkin pie to make the night complete.

- **Sandwich Potluck**—Everyone on your guest list brings sandwich makings and other lunch items for a build-your-own-sandwich event. This is perfect for your friends who don't know how to turn on their ovens. Of course, even they could find success in whipping up a batch of our tasty tuna fish or chicken salad.

- **Luncheon Potluck**—Select something delicious like low-fat chicken parmesan or lemon baked fish for your friends to enjoy without guilt.

But the best idea of all might be to pore through this cookbook and select some tried-and-true dishes.

Share these recipes with your family too. They'll absolutely love you for it.

Linda Evans Shepherd and Eva Marie Everson

# A Child's Potluck

Let me explain something right off: potlucks and the South are synonymous. I grew up experiencing "dinner on the grounds" at church, family reunions (including some where I thought, *Do I know any of these people?*), and neighborhood gatherings held at the local park that was built in the dip between the "Big Lake" and the highway.

There was always a woman who appeared in charge. She spotted the other ladies descending from their cars, covered dishes in hand, and then pointed to the places on the picnic tables where that particular dish should go. Most of the women spent their lives in the kitchen, cooking up some of the most delectable dishes anyone ever let slip between their lips. Banana cream pies, homemade pound cakes, fried chicken that (as we say) made you want to slap your mama, vegetable casseroles, sweet salads, and the list goes on and on.

There were also the women who couldn't care less about the kitchen. These were the ladies who brought deviled eggs served on the deviled egg platters they'd received as wedding gifts, iced tea (always sweet), or the paper plates and plastic utensils. Their vegetable dishes were simple: throw some green beans in a pot, add a little bacon fat, bring to a boil, let simmer, serve.

While women were placing their goods on cement tables and exchanging recipes ("Oh, that looks *so good*! You must give me the recipe!"), the men stood in clusters, talking about their jobs, hunting, fishing, or baseball. We children ran freely between the playground equipment—the swings, the monkey bars, and the giant silvery slide—until the woman in charge called out that dinner was ready. Then, sweaty and hungry, we joined our parents. A pastor—for there was always one in attendance—prayed the blessing, and the potluck was served.

Eva Marie

# *Potluck* Snack Attack

## APPETIZERS

A favorite recipe for the gang on football Sundays. The number of servings will depend on the size of the meatballs.

# Eva's Sausage Balls

3 cups  Bisquick mix

1 lb.  ground sausage, room temperature

10 oz.  cheddar cheese, grated

Mix first two ingredients well. Add cheese and mix until dry ingredients are moist and will roll into balls. Bake in a 350° oven until brown.

# Mom's Cereal Snacks

| | |
|---|---|
| ½ stick | margarine or butter, melted |
| ½ cup | oil |
| 3 Tbsp. | Worcestershire sauce |
| 2–3 Tbsp. | Tabasco |
| 2 Tbsp. | liquid smoke |
| 1 tsp. | garlic powder |
| 1 tsp. | onion powder |
| 1 tsp. | seasoned salt |
| 4–6 cups | Corn Chex |
| 4–6 cups | Rice Chex |
| 4–6 cups | Traditional Chex Mix |
| 2 cups | cheese/fish crackers |
| 2 cups | small pretzels |
| 1 cup | mixed nuts |
| 1 cup | cashew nuts |
| 2 cups | pecans |
| 1 cup | peanuts |
| 1 cup | almonds |

*Linda*

My dear mom has experimented with this recipe for the last forty years. And you know, I think she finally got it right! This snack is unbelievably delicious and totally addictive.

In 1-quart glass measuring cup, melt butter, add oil, Worcestershire sauce, Tabasco, and liquid smoke and stir. Next add garlic powder, onion powder, and seasoned salt and stir well.

In large container, mix all dry ingredients: Chex, crackers, pretzels, and nuts.

Pour liquid mixture over dry ingredients, 1 tablespoon at a time, and stir. Bake in one large pan or two smaller pans at 275° for one hour, stirring every 15 minutes. Pour out onto paper towels (over newspaper) to cool and absorb excess oil.

Yield: 22 to 28 cups. Great for gift giving.

My husband brought this recipe home after an office party where, he says, it was the hit. One taste and you'll know why.

# Vegetable Dip

| | |
|---|---|
| 1 cup | mayonnaise |
| 1 cup | sour cream |
| ½ cup | parsley, chopped |
| 2 Tbsp. | onion, minced |
| 1 Tbsp. | Dijon mustard |
| 1 clove | garlic, minced |
| 1 tsp. | salt |

In a medium bowl, stir together mayonnaise, sour cream, parsley, onion, mustard, garlic, and salt. Cover and chill at least 1 hour. Serve as dip with carrots, celery, zucchini, yellow crookneck squash, mushrooms, cauliflower, etc.

# Linda's Caramel Ritz Bits Crackers

| | |
|---|---|
| 2 (9 oz.) boxes | Ritz Bits crackers |
| 1 cup | dry-roasted peanuts |
| ½ cup | butter |
| 1 cup | sugar |
| ½ cup | corn syrup |
| 1 tsp. | vanilla |
| 1 tsp. | baking soda |

Combine in greased, large, shallow baking pan 2 boxes of crackers and peanuts. Then, in saucepan, melt butter, add sugar and syrup, and bring to a boil. Cook 5 minutes. Remove pan from heat; stir in vanilla and baking soda.

Pour caramel mixture over crackers and nuts; stir well. Bake one hour in 250° oven, stirring every 15 minutes. Pour onto waxed paper and break apart. Allow to cool. Store in airtight container.

Yield: 9 cups of snack mix.

*Linda*

These should come with a warning: dangerous snack—be sure you're not left alone with a fresh batch.

I love stuffed mushrooms. I could eat them until I'm silly.

# Sausage-Stuffed Mushrooms

| | |
|---:|---|
| 1 lb. | fresh large mushrooms |
| 1 lb. | fresh pork sausage |
| 1 tsp. | garlic, minced |
| 2 Tbsp. | parsley, chopped |
| 1½ cups | sharp Cheddar cheese, shredded |

Rinse mushrooms and pat dry. Remove stems. Chop stems and combine with sausage, garlic, and parsley. Cook sausage mixture until browned, stirring to crumble. Drain off drippings. Stir in cheese. Mix well. Spoon mixture into mushroom caps and place in a 9-by-13 baking dish. Bake at 350° for 20 minutes.

Yield: 2 dozen.

# Avocado Dip

| | |
|---:|:---|
| 16 oz. | sour cream |
| 1 package | Hidden Valley Party Dip mix |
| 2 | ripe avocados |
| 2 Tbsp. | lemon juice |
| 1 | small onion |
| 2 | jalapeño peppers |
| | salt, to taste |

Mix sour cream and party dip mix. Blend together in blender: avocados, lemon juice, onion, jalapeño peppers, and pinch of salt. (You can add a tablespoon of sour cream if more liquid is needed in blender.) Blend well. Add to sour cream mix. Stir well. Chill.

Serves a bag of chips well.

*Linda*

If you like spicy guacamole, you'll love this. Great for picnics, potlucks, and Super Bowl parties.

## Snowy Snack Mix

I was given a tin of this homemade delectable as a Christmas gift one year. The giver included the recipe, and it's been a favorite ever since. It's perfect for a teen party or adult social.

| | |
|---|---|
| 12 oz. | semisweet chocolate chips |
| 1 cup | peanut butter |
| 12 oz. | box Golden Grahams cereal |
| 16 oz. | peanuts |
| 1 cup | raisins |
| | (alternative: ½ cup dark raisins and ½ cup golden raisins) |
| 1 box | confectioners' sugar |

Melt chocolate and peanut butter together. Mix cereal, nuts, and raisins. Pour chocolate mixture over this and coat well. Put in paper bag with confectioners' sugar and shake to coat well. Pour into large bowl and watch it disappear!

# Porcupine Meatballs

| | |
|---|---|
| 1 ½ lbs. | ground beef |
| ½ cup | uncooked long-grain rice |
| 2 tsp. | salt |
| 1 can | Campbell's tomato soup |
| 1 can | water |
| 1 | onion, chopped finely |
| 1 | bell pepper, chopped finely |
| | garlic (optional) |
| | chopped jalapeño pepper (optional) |

Mix beef, rice, and salt and roll mixture loosely into balls (so rice will fluff).

In a separate pan, mix soup, water, onion, pepper, garlic, and hot pepper (optional). Simmer for 15 minutes. Drop meatballs into mixture then simmer for 1 ½ hours on stovetop, stirring occasionally to keep meatballs from sticking to the pan.

**Optional:** bake the meatballs in the sauce in a greased casserole dish for 1 ½ hours in an oven set at 350°.

Yield: approximately 3 dozen meatballs.

*Linda*

This recipe came into my collection from my aunt Frances, and the reason it's called "porcupine" is because of the way the rice sticks out of each meatball. This is great served as a main dish with vegetables.

# Mom's Cornbread Casserole

My mom has always been the hero of her kitchen, a great recipe huntress who's sampled and traded recipes with the best cooks at her PTA meetings, office potlucks, and our church potluck suppers. When I was a child, she'd stay up on the latest casseroles and the most exciting desserts that were making the rounds in the homes of our town's best cooks. My little brother and I grew up sampling her fabulous finds, which often contained ingredients such as Cheese Whiz, Cool Whip, and Campbell's cream of mushroom soup.

One Sunday, Mom pulled her first-ever batch of cornbread casserole from the oven. After the prayer, my family and I heaped our plates with salad, beef, and cheesy potatoes. Then we added a thick slice of the steaming cornbread to our plates.

The cornbread was so good, made with real corn and jalapeños. My mother radiated with excitement. "Jane brought a batch of this dish to our office potluck last Friday, and when I tasted it, I knew I had to get the recipe. There was a little something missing, so I added a few hot peppers. Tell me what you think."

We heaped our praises on Mom and encouraged her to bring her cornbread to our next family reunion, which was to be held at the picnic tables beside an ancient East Texas graveyard, the final resting place of several members of my dad's family.

On this broiling July day, Mom proudly placed her cornbread casserole next to chicken baked in mushroom soup, ice-cold watermelon, Butterfinger cake, and the ever-present broccoli and green bean casseroles.

The aunts gathered around Mom to congratulate her on her potluck offering. "Verna, this is delicious! Can I have the recipe?"

Proudly, Mom gave each aunt a handwritten copy. The next year, when we arrived at the family reunion with yet another cornbread casserole in hand, we found it was only one of a dozen clones, all made from my mom's recipe.

Linda

# *Potluck* Kneads Dough

## BREADS

This is my dad's favorite! If you like it hot and spicy, add the hot pepper. Otherwise, it's pretty good without it.

# Mom's Cornbread Casserole

|  |  |
|---:|---|
| 1 | onion, chopped |
| ½ | green bell pepper, chopped |
|  | chopped hot pepper (optional) |
| 1 small jar | pimiento |
| 1 can | whole corn |
| 1 can | cream-style corn |
| 3 | eggs, lightly beaten |
| 1 (6 oz.) package | corn bread mix |
| ¾ stick | margarine, melted |

Mix together chopped onion, bell pepper, hot peppers (if desired), pimento, whole corn, cream-style corn, and add beaten eggs. Stir in corn bread mix. Add melted margarine. Pour into greased casserole dish and bake at 375° for 45–50 minutes or until done in center. (You can double this recipe and freeze half, if desired.)

Serves 9–12.

# Buttermilk Biscuits

| | |
|---:|---|
| ¾ cup | butter, softened |
| 3 cups | all-purpose flour |
| 4½ tsp. | baking powder |
| ¾ tsp. | baking soda |
| ¾ tsp. | salt |
| 1 | egg |
| ¾ cup | buttermilk |

In a bowl, mix butter into dry ingredients. When fully combined, stir in the egg and buttermilk until the mixture forms a ball of dough. Roll and cut into ¾ inch thickness with a 2½ inch diameter cookie cutter. Bake in a preheated 400° oven for 15 minutes.

Yield: approximately 18 mouth-watering biscuits.

*Eva Marie*

A Southern tradition from every woman's cookbook is buttermilk biscuits. And, by the way, use butter—not margarine!

Wanna break away from the ordinary muffin? Impress your taste buds with these. Great for brunches.

## Linda's Pecan Pie Mini Muffins

| | |
|---|---|
| 1 cup | brown sugar, packed |
| ½ cup | flour |
| 1 cup | chopped pecans |
| ⅔ cup | butter (no substitutes), melted |
| 2 | eggs |

Combine brown sugar, flour, and pecans. Combine butter and eggs in separate bowl. Stir into flour mixture. Fill mini-muffin tins ⅔ full. Bake at 350° for 10–12 minutes. Remove immediately.

Serves approximately 12.

# Old-fashioned Corn Bread

| | |
|---:|:---|
| 1 ½ cups | yellow corn meal |
| ¾ tsp. | baking soda |
| 1 tsp. | salt |
| 1 ⅓ cups | buttermilk |
| 2 | eggs, separated |
| ¼ cup | shortening, melted |

Sift corn meal, soda, and salt together. Add buttermilk to well-beaten egg yolks and add to corn meal mixture; beat well. Add hot melted shortening and again beat well. Fold in stiffly beaten egg whites. Turn immediately into a piping hot, greased, heavy 10-inch skillet. Bake in a preheated 450° oven for 25–30 minutes. Serve at once with butter.

*Eva Marie*

This recipe is the perfect complement to a big pot of homemade vegetable soup on a wintry day.

# Mother's Upside-Down Cake

When I was growing up, my family attended our small town's Methodist church located at the end of Main Street. I fondly remember Mother's monthly Methodist women's "Circle Meetings" and all that they held in store . . . for me.

If the meetings were held at another member's home, Mother would prepare some delectable dish perfect for such a gathering. Finger foods, mostly. Cute little sandwiches, easy-to-serve salads, and such. After the food was prepared, she would take a bath, give her face a little pat of powdered rouge, apply some red lipstick, dab on perfume, put on a pretty dress and gloves, slip her feet into some extremely spiky high heels, and off she'd go.

But if the meeting was held at our house, she'd spend the morning covering the dining room table with fine linen and bringing out her "good china" and crystal. She'd polish the furniture and fret a bit over the rest of the house. Then she'd take her bath and get dressed.

One day, one such meeting was being held in our home. She made a cake that morning—a delicious, three-layer yellow cake with homemade chocolate frosting. She placed it on a serving dish and then placed the serving dish on top of the refrigerator, away from little hands and eyes. Then she left us—my younger brother and me—unattended, just long enough to take the bath.

And just long enough for the two of us—ages five and two—to drag a kitchen chair over to the counter. While my brother held the chair, I stood on its seat. Carefully, oh so carefully, I stepped onto the counter, where I had a perfect view of the dessert. I thought if I stole a finger's worth of the icing, no one would be the wiser. Mission accomplished, but then I heard Mother coming out of the bathroom. Startled, I moved too quickly, sending the cake to the floor, where it landed upside down and with a splat.

I don't remember a lot about the rest of that day. I do remember Mother, smelling like talcum powder and dressed in a slip, scraping cake off the floor and declaring she didn't know what had gotten into me. And, as I also recall, there was no cake served to the ladies of the "Circle" that day.

Children and cakes should never be left alone to fend for themselves.

Eva Marie

# *Potluck* Cake Walk

## CAKES, COOKIES, AND ICINGS

This is one of my husband's very favorite cakes!

# Paul's Favorite Chocolate Cherry Cake

| | |
|---|---|
| 1 package | fudge cake mix |
| 1 can | cherry pie filling |
| 2 | eggs |
| 1 Tbsp. | almond flavoring |

Stir together cake mix, pie filling, eggs, and flavoring. Pour mixture into a greased 9-by-13 pan and bake at 350° for 30–35 minutes.

| | |
|---|---|
| 1 cup | sugar |
| 5 Tbsp. | butter |
| ⅓ cup | milk |
| 1 cup | chocolate chips |
| ½ cup | chopped toasted pecans or walnuts (optional) |

Boil sugar, butter, and milk in a saucepan for 1½ minutes. Add chocolate chips, stir until melted, and pour over hot cake. Sprinkle with toasted pecans or walnuts if desired.

# Almond Chocolate Biscotti

| 1 package | chocolate cake mix |
| 1 cup | all-purpose flour |
| ½ cup | butter or margarine, melted (butter is best) |
| ¼ cup | chocolate syrup |
| 2 | eggs |
| ½ tsp. | almond extract |
| ½ cup | slivered almonds |
| ½ cup | mini semisweet chocolate chips |
| 1 package | vanilla chips |
| 2 Tbsp. | shortening |

In a large mixing bowl, combine dry cake mix, flour, butter, chocolate syrup, eggs, and extract. Mix well. Stir in the almonds and miniature chocolate chips. Divide dough in half. On ungreased baking sheets, shape each portion into a 12-by-2-inch log.

Bake at 350° for 30–35 minutes or until firm to the touch. Cool for 15–30 minutes. Transfer to a cutting board; carefully cut diagonally with a serrated knife into ½ inch slices. Place cut side down on ungreased baking sheets. Bake for another 10–15 minutes or until firm. Remove to wire racks to cool.

For dipping: in a small heavy saucepan over low heat, melt vanilla chips and shortening. Drizzle over biscotti (or dip one side in); let stand until hardened. Store in an airtight container.

*Eva Marie*

My friend Carin gifted an editor friend with the makings of this recipe. Then, on a business trip, my editor friend and I ate 'em up!

If you like moist cranberry cookies as much as I do, give these a try!

# Cranberry Cookies

| | |
|---|---|
| 1 cup | butter, softened |
| ½ cup | sugar |
| 2 Tbsp. | milk |
| 1 tsp. | vanilla |
| 2 ½ cups | sifted flour |
| ½ tsp. | salt |
| ½ cup | pecans, finely chopped |
| ¾ cup | dried cranberries |
| ¾ cup | coconut |

In mixing bowl, cream butter until light and creamy and slowly add sugar. Gradually mix in milk, vanilla, flour, and salt to butter/sugar mixture. Lightly beat. Next add pecans and cranberries.

Form cookie dough into two logs. Brush dough logs with a little water. Roll logs into coconut, pressing lightly so coconut will stick to sides. Chill 2 hours. Slice thin with serrated knife. Bake at 375° for 12 minutes until edges are golden.

## Apricot White Chocolate Biscotti

| | |
|---|---|
| 1 | yellow cake mix |
| 1 cup | all-purpose flour |
| ½ cup | butter, melted |
| 2 | eggs |
| 1 ½ tsp. | vanilla extract |
| ½ cup | miniature white chocolate chips |
| ½ cup | dried apricot, chopped small |
| 1 package | Baker's white chocolate chips |
| 2 Tbsp. | shortening |

In a large mixing bowl, combine dry cake mix, flour, butter, eggs, and extract. Mix well. Stir in miniature white chocolate chips and fruit. (If the mixture comes out a little thick, add a couple Tbsp. milk.)

Divide dough in half. On ungreased baking sheets, shape each portion into a 12-by-2-inch log.

Bake at 350° for 30–35 minutes or until firm to the touch. Cool for 15–30 minutes. Transfer to a cutting board; carefully cut diagonally with a serrated knife into ½ inch slices. Place cut side down on ungreased baking sheets. Bake for another 10–15 minutes or until firm. Remove to wire racks to cool.

For dipping: in a small heavy saucepan over low heat, melt white chocolate and shortening. Dip edges of biscotti into the chocolate (only one side in); let stand until hardened. Store in an airtight container.

*Eva Marie*

Another recipe from Carin. I'm torn as to which one I like best!

## Verna's Butterfinger Cake

*Linda*

If you want to
make a cake
all your friends
will talk about,
try this one. I
guarantee it will
be a conversation
piece.

| | |
|---|---|
| 18.25 oz. box | yellow cake mix |
| 1 ¼ cups | water |
| ⅓ cup | vegetable oil |
| 3 | eggs |
| 1 (14 oz.) can | sweetened condensed milk |
| 6 | Butterfinger candy bars |
| 12 oz. container | Cool Whip |

Follow cake mix directions to blend cake mix, water, oil, and eggs, then bake cake (according to instructions) in a 9-by-13 inch pan. While still hot, punch holes in cake with an ice pick or butter knife. Pour ¾ can sweetened condensed milk over top of cake. Crush 3 Butterfingers and sprinkle over cake. When cool, spread 12 oz. Cool Whip over cake. Sprinkle with 3 more crushed Butterfinger bars. Refrigerate.

# Fudge Icing

| | |
|---|---|
| 2 cups | sugar |
| ⅓ cup | cocoa |
| ¼ tsp. | salt |
| ½ cup | milk |
| ½ cup | margarine |
| 1 tsp. | vanilla |

Combine first five ingredients and bring to a rolling boil. Boil two minutes. Remove from stove and, when cooled, beat and add vanilla.

*Eva Marie*

I've always believed that a great cake deserves the best icing.

Linda

I made this recipe as a child with my mom, and I've made it with my own children. I still make it with my disabled daughter because it's all stir and no bake.

# Thingamajig Oatmeal Cookies

| | |
|---|---|
| 2 cups | sugar |
| 1 stick | margarine |
| ¼ cup | cocoa |
| ½ cup | milk |
| ⅔ cup | peanut butter (chunky is excellent) |
| 2 tsp. | vanilla |
| ½ cup | peanuts, chopped |
| 3 cups | rolled oats |
| 1 cup | miniature marshmallows |

Bring sugar, margarine, cocoa, and milk to a boil for one minute on top of stove. Remove from heat and add peanut butter, vanilla, and peanuts. Stir until peanut butter is dissolved. Stir in rolled oats then add marshmallows. Mix well. Drop mixture on waxed paper by teaspoon.

Yield: approximately 50–60 small cookies.

## Mayonnaise Cake

| | |
|---|---|
| 2 cups | flour |
| 1 cup | sugar |
| 4 Tbsp. | cocoa |
| 1 ½ tsp. | baking powder |
| | pinch of salt |
| 1 ½ tsp. | baking soda |
| 1 cup | mayonnaise (do not use low-fat) |
| 1 cup | water |
| 2 tsp. | vanilla |

Mix flour, sugar, cocoa, baking powder, salt, and baking soda together. Add mayonnaise, water, and vanilla. Do not overstir. Bake in 2 9-inch pans in 350° oven for 25–30 minutes.

Linda

This is a nice moist chocolate cake. Try one of Eva's icing recipes to top it off.

This is the perfect topping for an angel or sponge cake—or Linda's mayonnaise cake.

# Chocolate Nut Fluff Frosting

| | |
|---|---|
| ½ cup | halved, blanched* almonds |
| 1 ½ Tbsp. | butter |
| 1 cup | semisweet chocolate |
| 2 cups | heavy cream, whipped |

Cook almonds in butter until golden. Remove from stovetop and cool. Melt chocolate pieces in top of double boiler over hot water. Cool to room temperature. Fold chocolate and almonds into whipped cream, allowing chocolate to harden in flecks. Frost angel or sponge cake.

* Blanching almonds is easy and takes no more than five minutes. Here's what you do:

Boil enough water to cover the amount of almonds you have when the almonds are in a bowl.

Place the almonds in a bowl.

Pour boiling water over almonds just enough to cover them.

Allow almonds to sit for exactly one minute.

Drain, rinse under cold water, drain again.

Pat them dry and then slip the skins off.

# German Sweet Chocolate Cake and Frosting

| | |
|---|---|
| 1 package | Baker's German sweet chocolate |
| ½ cup | boiling water |
| 1 cup | butter |
| 2 cups | sugar |
| 4 | egg yolks, unbeaten |
| 1 tsp. | vanilla |
| ½ tsp. | salt |
| 1 tsp. | baking soda |
| 2½ cups | sifted cake flour (I prefer Swans Down) |
| 1 cup | buttermilk |
| 4 | egg whites, stiffly beaten |

*Eva Marie*

This recipe takes a little time, but it is oh-so-worth the effort! German chocolate cake gets me to the dessert table every time.

Preheat oven to 350°. Melt chocolate in boiling water. Let cool. Cream butter and sugar until fluffy. Add egg yolks, one yolk at a time. (Beat well after each.) Add melted chocolate and vanilla. Mix well. Sift together salt, baking soda, and flour. Add alternately with buttermilk to chocolate mixture, beating well. Beat until smooth. Fold in beaten egg whites. Pour into 3 8- or 9-inch cake layer pans, greased and lined on bottom with waxed paper. Bake for 30–40 minutes. Allow to cool before frosting top only.

### Frosting Ingredients

| | | | | |
|---|---|---|---|---|
| 1 cup | evaporated milk | | 1 tsp. | vanilla |
| 1 cup | sugar | | 1½ cups | Baker's Angel Flake coconut |
| 3 | egg yolks | | | |
| ¼ lb. | margarine | | 1 cup | pecans, chopped |

Combine milk, sugar, egg yolks, margarine, and vanilla. Cook and stir over medium heat until thickened, about 12 minutes. Add coconut and pecans. Beat until thick enough to spread. Makes about 2⅔ cups, enough for top only.

# Strawberry Shortcut Cake

**Linda**

My grandparents grew strawberries every summer and served strawberry shortcake all year long. Here's a great recipe that reminds me of my grandmother's wonderful dessert.

| | |
|---:|---|
| 2 ½ cups | miniature marshmallows |
| 4 cups | strawberries, mashed |
| 3 oz. package | strawberry-flavored Jell-O gelatin |
| 1 | white or yellow cake mix |
| | oil, water, and eggs per package instructions |
| | whipped cream or topping (optional) |

Heat oven to 350°. Generously grease a 9-by-13 pan. Sprinkle marshmallows over bottom of pan. In a bowl, combine mashed strawberries and gelatin then set aside. Make cake batter according to the package directions. Spread batter over marshmallows in pan. Spoon strawberry mixture evenly over batter. Bake for 35–45 minutes or until toothpick inserted in center comes out clean. Place cake on a wire rack to cool. When cake has cooled completely, cut and serve inverted or invert onto a large serving plate or foil-covered board or square of cardboard. Cut into squares and serve with whipped cream or whipped topping.

# Italian Coconut Cream Cake

| | |
|---|---|
| 2 cups | sugar |
| 5 | egg yolks (save whites) |
| 2 sticks | butter |
| 2 cups | plain flour |
| 1 cup | buttermilk |
| 1 cup | pecans, chopped |
| ¼ tsp. | salt |
| 1 tsp. | baking soda |
| 1 tsp. | vanilla |
| 2 cups | Angel Flake coconut |

*Eva Marie*

Marvelous for summer picnics. My mother said she hasn't made this in a while, but she always loved Italian coconut cream cake.

Preheat oven to 350°. Cream sugar, egg yolks, and butter together. Add all other ingredients except egg whites and beat well. Beat egg whites until stiff and fold into mixture. Bake for 30–35 minutes. (Use 3 9-inch pans.) Frost with icing (below).

### Icing Ingredients

| | |
|---|---|
| 8 oz. | cream cheese |
| 1 stick | margarine |
| 1 box | powdered sugar |
| 1 tsp. | vanilla |
| | coconut |

Cream cream cheese, margarine, and powdered sugar together until smooth. Add vanilla. Spread on cake layers. Sprinkle additional coconut between layers and on top.

# Butterscotch Brownies

**Linda**

This was one of the first treats I learned to make as a child. These moist brownies have an amazing flavor.

| | |
|---|---|
| 1 ½ cups | margarine |
| 2 cups | brown sugar |
| 2 | eggs |
| 1 ½ cups | flour, sifted |
| 2 tsp. | baking powder |
| 1 tsp. | salt |
| 1 tsp. | vanilla |
| 1 cup | chopped nuts |

Heat oven to 325°. Melt margarine over low heat. Set aside. In mixing bowl, blend in sugar and eggs, then add melted margarine. In separate bowl, sift together flour, baking powder, salt, and stir into mixing bowl. Add vanilla and nuts. Spread dough into a well-greased and floured 9-by-9 pan. Bake 20–25 minutes. While warm, cut into squares.

## Grandmother Miller's Tea Cakes

| | |
|---|---|
| 1 stick | butter |
| 1 | egg |
| 1 cup | sugar |
| 2 Tbsp. | milk |
| 1 tsp. | vanilla |
| 2¾ cups | self-rising flour |

Preheat oven to 375°. Cream butter, egg, sugar, milk, and vanilla. Sift flour. Add to creamed mixture. Chill at least three hours. Roll and cut out your favorite size cookie. Bake for about eight minutes, keeping a watch through the oven window.

Yield: 60 cookies.

*Eva Marie*

A family member (once or twice removed) gave me a recipe for tea cakes years ago. Since then, I have found making tea cakes a fun and simple thing to do.

# Merry Potluck

I'm usually too busy to host my Christmas party until February. That's when my hubby and I send out our annual "White Elephant Christmas Party and Potluck" invitations, inviting guests to bring a dish as well as a wrapped gift. This means that just like Forrest Gump and his box of chocolates, nobody knows what they're going to get until they've walked through our buffet line and unwrapped a present from beneath our Christmas tree.

When the night arrives, each guest secretly places a present under our still-sparkling tree before heading for our eight-foot-long kitchen island, which we've nicknamed "Potluck Island." As our friends add their homemade treats to our ever-expanding bounty, the party starts. Next to a stack of red paper Christmas plates are homemade cookies, taco casserole, Texas barbecued chicken in a Crock-Pot, and the ever-present pan of brownies.

I help the small children make their selections and giggle when the ladies exclaim over their loaded plates, "How did I get so much food? I only took a little of everything. Now I look like a pig!"

The men forego these guilty explanations and soon come back for a heaping second helping. We eat, we laugh, we open presents, and we celebrate the spirit of Christmas even though the holiday is still ten months away.

Linda

# *Potluck* Crock-Pots

## CROCK-POT MEALS

# Texas Barbecued Chicken in a Crock-Pot

*Linda*

If you like barbecued chicken as much as we do, try this quick and easy recipe.

| 3–6 | boneless, skinless chicken breasts |
| 2 cups | tomato ketchup |
| 3 Tbsp. | brown sugar |
| 1 Tbsp. | Worcestershire sauce |
| 1 Tbsp. | soy sauce |
| 1 Tbsp. | cider vinegar |
| ¼ cup | water |
| 1 tsp. | pepper, or to taste |
| ½ tsp. | garlic powder |

Combine all ingredients except chicken in the Crock-Pot. Next, add chicken, coating all sides with the sauce. Cover and cook chicken on high for 3–4 hours. When chicken is thoroughly cooked, remove from pot and cut in bite-sized chunks or shred. Put chicken back into pot and stir into sauce. Keep Crock-Pot on low until ready to serve. This is good over rolls or cooked rice.

Serves 5–9.

# Turkey Chili

*Eva Marie*

This is a great way to keep the red meat out of an all-time favorite in our household.

| | |
|---|---|
| 1 | medium onion, chopped (should yield about ½ cup) |
| 1 clove | garlic, finely chopped |
| 2 tsp. | ground cumin |
| ⅛ tsp. | ground red cayenne pepper |
| 1 (15.5 oz.) can | great northern beans, drained |
| 1 (15 oz.) can | dark red kidney beans, drained |
| 2 (4.5 oz.) cans | chopped green chilies, undrained |
| 2 (14 oz.) cans | chicken broth |
| 2 lbs. | turkey thighs, skin removed |
| 1 cup | frozen shoepeg white corn (from 1 lb. bag), thawed |
| 2 Tbsp. | all-purpose flour |
| ¼ cup | water |
| 1 | lime, cut into wedges (optional) |

In 4–5 quart Crock-Pot, mix all ingredients except turkey, corn, flour, water, and lime. Then place turkey in bean mixture. Cover. Cook on low setting 8–10 hours.

Place turkey on cutting board. Remove meat from bones, discard bones. Cut turkey into bite-size pieces. Add turkey and corn to cooker. In small bowl, mix flour and water. Stir into turkey mixture. Increase heat setting to high. Cover and cook one half hour. Mixture will be slightly thick. Serve with lime wedges for squeezing juice over chili.

Serves 6 at 1½ cups each.

## Mary's Slow Cooker Lasagna

Linda

I have to thank my sister-in-law, Mary, for this delightful dish. Delicious!

| | |
|---:|---|
| 1 lb. | ground chuck |
| 1 tsp. | Italian seasoning |
| 1 (28 oz.) can | Hunt's spaghetti sauce |
| ⅓ cup | water |
| 8 | lasagna noodles, uncooked |
| 1 (15 oz.) carton | ricotta cheese |
| 2 cups | shredded part-skim mozzarella cheese, divided |

Cook beef and Italian seasoning over medium-high heat, stirring until beef crumbles. Drain. Combine spaghetti sauce and water in small bowl. Place 4 uncooked noodles in bottom of a lightly greased 5-quart electric slow cooker. Layer with half each of beef mixture, spaghetti sauce mixture. Spread in ricotta cheese. Sprinkle with one cup mozzarella cheese. Layer with remaining noodles, meat, sauce mixture, and mozzarella cheese. Cover and cook on high setting 1 hour. Reduce heat and cook on low setting 5 hours.

# Barbecue Beef

| | |
|---|---|
| 3 to 4 lbs. | boneless beef chuck roast |
| | salt and pepper to taste |
| ¾ cup | barbecue sauce |
| ¼ cup | orange marmalade |
| 1 Tbsp. | vinegar |
| 2 Tbsp. | cornstarch |
| 2 Tbsp. | water |

Place first five ingredients in Crock-Pot. Cook on low for 5 hours. Separate meat from sauce.

Add 2 tablespoons cornstarch and 2 tablespoons water. Heat in Crock-Pot on low until thick. Mix with meat. Serves well with rice and corn on the cob.

*Eva Marie*

This recipe came from my friend Gayle, whose handwriting appeared on some of the recipe cards in our Potluck Club novels.

# Chicken Cacciatore

*Linda*

Imagine this: you've just walked into your kitchen with a bubbling Crock-Pot full of chicken cacciatore all ready to serve! Follow this recipe and you could make it happen.

|  |  |
|---:|---|
| 1 | large onion, thinly sliced |
| 3 lbs. | chicken |
| 2 (6 oz.) cans | tomato paste |
| 4 oz. | sliced mushrooms |
| 1 tsp. | salt |
| 1–2 cloves | garlic, minced |
| 2 tsp. | oregano |
| ½ tsp. | celery seed |
| 1 | bay leaf |
| ¾ cup | water |

Place sliced onions in bottom of Crock-Pot. Cut up chicken and layer on top of onions. Stir together remaining ingredients. Pour over chicken. Cook on low 7–9 hours or high 3–4 hours. Serve over spaghetti or rice.

# Dumplings

| | |
|---|---|
| 1 ¼ cups | flour |
| 2 tsp. | baking powder |
| 1 tsp. | salt |
| 1 | egg, beaten |
| ⅔ to ¾ cup | milk |
| 1 Tbsp. | dried parsley flakes |

Turn Crock-Pot (containing your soup or stew) to high while preparing dumplings.

Mix flour, baking powder, and salt. Beat in egg and milk. Drop by teaspoonfuls in simmering stew or liquid. Sprinkle with parsley. Cover and cook on high 1 hour. Turn to low until serving time, if desired. Will hold well for 1–2 hours.

*Eva Marie*

This recipe goes with beef stew or with chicken in a pot.

# Chicken in a Pot

Well, here you
have it: chicken
in a pot.

| | |
|---:|:---|
| 1 3-lb. | chicken, whole or pieces |
| 2 | carrots, sliced |
| 2 | onions, sliced |
| 2 | celery stalks cut in 1-inch pieces |
| 2 tsp. | salt |
| ½ tsp. | black pepper |
| ½ cup | water or chicken broth |
| ½ to 1 tsp. | basil |

Place carrots, onions, and celery in bottom of Crock-Pot. Add whole chicken. Top with salt, pepper, liquid. Sprinkle basil over top. Cover and cook until done on low setting for 7–10 hours. Remove chicken and vegetables with spatula.

# Sloppy Joes from a Crock-Pot

|  |  |
|---|---|
| 3 lbs. | lean ground beef |
| 1 | large onion, chopped, about 1 cup |
| 1 cup | celery, chopped |
| ½ cup | green pepper, chopped |
| 1 (12 oz.) bottle | prepared chili sauce |
| 1 (6 oz.) can | tomato paste |
| 2–3 Tbsp. | brown sugar, to taste |
| 1–2 Tbsp. | Worcestershire sauce |
| ¼ tsp. | ground black pepper |
|  | toasted sandwich buns |

In large, deep skillet, brown ground beef along with onions, celery, and green pepper. Drain fat. Transfer the ground beef mixture to the Crock-Pot then stir in chili sauce, tomato paste, brown sugar, Worcestershire sauce, and pepper. Cover and cook on low for 4–5 hours, stirring occasionally. Serve meat mixture on toasted sandwich buns.

Serves 20.

*Linda*

Need a quick meal for a child's birthday party or potluck? I know from experience this is a hit.

Anyone who knows me knows I don't like to cook. But I never met a Crock-Pot I didn't swoon over. Here's an easy but delicious recipe to prove it.

# Stuffed Green Peppers

| | |
|---:|:---|
| 6 | small green peppers, tops removed and seeded |
| 1 lb. | ground beef or chuck |
| ⅔ cup | water |
| ½ cup | onion, chopped |
| ½ tsp. | salt |
| ¼ cup | ketchup |
| 1 cup | ketchup |
| ½ cup | water |
| 4 | carrots, peeled and cut in 3-inch pieces |
| ⅓ cup | raw rice (converted) |

Wash green peppers; drain well. Salt cavity lightly. Combine in medium bowl meat, ⅔ cup water, onion, salt, and ¼ cup ketchup. Mix well. Stuff green peppers ⅔ full. Arrange stuffed peppers in Crock-Pot (may be stacked) with carrot pieces to help support peppers. Pour in 1 cup ketchup and ½ cup water. Cover and cook on low for 6–8 hours. (If on high, reduce time to 3 hours.) Serve on a bed of rice and pour remaining tomato sauce over top.

# Crock-Pot of Spanish Rice

| | |
|---|---|
| 2 lbs. | lean ground beef |
| 1 cup | onion, chopped |
| 2 | green bell peppers, chopped |
| 1 (28 oz.) can | tomatoes |
| 1 (8 oz.) can | tomato sauce |
| 2½ tsp. | chili powder |
| 1½ tsp. | salt |
| 2 tsp. | Worcestershire sauce |
| 1 cup | rice, uncooked |
| 1 cup | water |

Brown beef in skillet; drain off fat. Combine all ingredients in slow cooker, stirring to blend well. Cover and cook on low for 6½–8 hours, or high for 3–3½ hours, or until rice is done. Do not use quick rice.

Serves 8.

*Linda*

This dish is always a hit at home.

Did I mention how much I like it "easy" in the kitchen?

# Crock-Pot Meat Loaf

| | |
|---|---|
| 1 lb. | extra lean ground beef |
| ¼ lb. | sausage meat |
| 1 | egg |
| 2 | slices of bread torn into soft crumbs |
| 1 | onion, chopped |
| 3 Tbsp. | parsley, chopped |
| ½ tsp. | ground black pepper |
| | Worcestershire sauce and Tabasco sauce (a few drops) |

Combine all ingredients and gently shape into a round loaf. Place on a trivet in Crock-Pot. Cover and cook on low, about 7–8 hours. Serve with tomato, barbecue, or chili sauce.

**Great idea:** chill leftovers and slice for sandwiches the next day.

# Linda's Spaghetti in a Crock-Pot

| | |
|---|---|
| 2 lbs. | hamburger |
| 18 oz. | spaghetti sauce |
| 1 (6 oz.) can | tomato paste |
| 1 | green pepper, sliced thin |
| 1 | large onion, sliced thin |
| ¼ cup | Parmesan cheese |
| 1 tsp. | parsley flakes |
| 1 cup | water |
| 1 Tbsp. | Parmesan cheese |

Brown hamburger in skillet, then drain.

In Crock-Pot, add spaghetti sauce, tomato paste, green pepper, onion, Parmesan, parsley, and water. Add browned hamburger. Cook on low 4 hours. Increase to high; cook 1 hour more. Serve over cooked spaghetti. Sprinkle with additional Parmesan.

*Linda*

Your family will love this easy, classic dish. My son could eat it every night.

# Hold the Calories, Please

For the first thirty years of my life, no one ever thought to bring "light fare" to a potluck, a church supper, dinner on the grounds, or a family reunion. No one talked about losing a few pounds or their cardiologist's latest diet plan. No one asked about trans fat. No one even knew what trans fat was. No one counted calories or grams, and no one said anything about carbs and white sugars.

Not so anymore. Everyone wants a way to cut a calorie.

I remember well when this started. In the late eighties, suddenly potlucks meant bringing baked chicken along with the fried. It meant bringing sugar-free pies to serve next to the calorie-rich cakes.

I attended a brunch at a friend's home in which she served moist and delicious chocolate muffins, swearing they were a healthy choice. When everyone had left I asked, "Just what was in those muffins?"

"Easy as anything," she said. "Take one chocolate cake mix, add one can of pumpkin pie, about a third of the can of water, stir, pour into muffin tins, bake according to the cake's recipe, and you're done."

These muffins are practically a staple in my kitchen now. I must warn you—if you try this recipe, remember if you overeat a healthy-choice food, the healthy *choice* is no longer a *healthy* choice.

Eva Marie

# *Potluck* Lightens Up

## COOKING LITE

# Seared Salmon on Herbed Mashed Peas

This recipe is fresh
and different.
And I dearly
love salmon!

| | |
|---:|:---|
| 1 tsp. | butter |
| 1 cup | leek, thinly sliced |
| ¼ cup | water |
| 1 (10 oz.) package | frozen green peas, thawed |
| 1 Tbsp. | fresh basil, chopped |
| 2 Tbsp. | fresh lemon juice |
| 2 tsp. | fresh tarragon, chopped |
| ½ tsp. | salt, divided |
| ½ tsp. | black pepper, divided |
| 4 (6 oz.) | salmon fillets |
| | cooking spray |

Heat butter in a medium nonstick skillet over medium heat. Add leek; cook 5 minutes or until tender, stirring occasionally. Add water and peas; cook 5 minutes or until peas are tender.

Place pea mixture in a food processor. Add basil, juice, and tarragon; process until smooth, adding more water if necessary. Stir in ¼ teaspoon salt and ¼ teaspoon pepper; keep mixture warm.

Sprinkle salmon with remaining ¼ teaspoon salt and remaining ¼ teaspoon pepper. Heat a nonstick skillet over medium-high heat. Coat pan with cooking spray. Add salmon, skin side down, and cook for 6 minutes or until golden. Turn and cook for 8 minutes or until fish flakes easily with a fork or until desired degree of doneness. Serve salmon over warm mashed peas.

## Low-Fat Corn Bread Tamale Pie

|  |  |
|---|---|
|  | vegetable cooking spray |
| 1 lb. | low-fat ground beef |
| 1 cup | onion, chopped |
| 1 cup | green pepper, chopped |
| 1 clove | garlic, minced |
| 1 (8 oz.) can | tomato sauce |
| 1 (12 oz.) can | whole-kernel corn, drained |
| 15 | ripe olives, sliced |
| 1 Tbsp. | sugar |
| 1 Tbsp. | chili powder |
| ⅛ tsp. | salt |
| ¼ tsp. | pepper |
| 1 cup | shredded reduced-fat sharp Cheddar cheese |
| ¾ cup | yellow cornmeal |
| ½ tsp. | salt |
| 2 cups | water |
| 1 Tbsp. | reduced-calorie margarine |

*Linda*

Enjoy this hearty, reduced-fat meal. It's a family favorite.

Coat nonstick skillet with cooking spray. Place over medium heat. Add ground beef, cook until brown. Drain on paper towels. Sauté onion, green pepper, and garlic until tender. Stir in ground beef, tomato sauce, corn, olives, sugar, chili powder, salt, and pepper. Simmer uncovered 15–20 minutes. Add Cheddar cheese, stirring until cheese melts. Spoon into 8-inch square baking dish coated with spray.

In separate saucepan, combine cornmeal, salt, water, and bring to boil, stirring constantly. Cook 3 minutes until thickened. Add margarine. Spoon over meat to within 1 inch of edge. Bake at 375° for 40 minutes.

Since my husband's "cardiac event," we're looking for ways to eat healthy. Here's one we enjoy.

# Flank Steak

| | |
|---|---|
| 2 Tbsp. | canola oil |
| 6 Tbsp. | concentrated chicken broth (lower sodium if available) |
| ½ cup | honey |
| ½ cup | lower-sodium soy sauce |
| 4 | green onions (the white and part of the green) cut into thin, diagonal slices |
| 1 tsp. | ground ginger (or 2 tsp. fresh minced ginger) |
| 1 tsp. | garlic powder (or 2 tsp. fresh minced garlic) |
| 2 tsp. | Worcestershire sauce |
| 1 | medium-large flank steak (about 1 ½ lbs.) |

Combine canola oil, chicken broth, honey, soy sauce, green onions, ginger, garlic powder, and Worcestershire sauce in a medium bowl with a whisk; set aside. Remove any visible fat from the flank. Lightly score the meat with a serrated knife, cutting about ¼-inch into the meat in a crisscross pattern (leave about an inch between cuts) on the top and bottom of the flank. Put the flank in a rectangular plastic container, add the marinade, and coat the steak well all over. Cover and marinate the flank steak all day or overnight, turning occasionally. Grill 10–15 minutes on each side or until cooked to desired doneness. Use a carving knife to cut diagonally across the grain of the meat into slices of your desired thickness.

Serves 6.

# Low-Fat Chicken Parmesan

|            |                                              |
|------------|----------------------------------------------|
| 4–5        | boneless chicken breasts                     |
| 1–2        | egg whites                                   |
| 1 cup      | corn flakes                                  |
|            | butter-flavored nonstick vegetable oil spray |
| 2 (8 oz.) cans | tomato sauce                             |
| 1½ tsp.    | oregano                                      |
| ½ tsp.     | basil                                        |
| ¼ tsp.     | thyme                                        |
| ¼ tsp.     | pepper                                       |
|            | Parmesan cheese, grated                      |
| 1 cup      | grated low-fat mozzarella cheese             |

Dip chicken in egg whites that have been slightly beaten and roll in corn flakes that have been crushed or processed in blender. Place chicken in a casserole dish that has been sprayed with butter-flavored nonstick vegetable oil spray. Pour tomato sauce into separate bowl, stir in oregano, basil, thyme, and pepper. Spoon sauce over chicken and top with the Parmesan cheese. Bake at 350° for 30 minutes. Top with mozzarella and bake an additional 15 minutes.

Serves 4–5.

*Linda*

All the flavor without the high calories. Delightful.

A Southern
delicacy
made light.

# Oven Barbecued Chicken

|          |                                       |
|----------|---------------------------------------|
| 3 lbs.   | chicken parts (choose your favorite)  |
| ¼ cup    | water                                 |
| ¼ cup    | vinegar                               |
| 3 Tbsp.  | oil                                   |
| ¼ cup    | chili sauce (or you can use ketchup)  |
| 3 Tbsp.  | Worcestershire sauce                  |
| 1 Tbsp.  | dry mustard                           |
| 1 ½ tsp. | salt                                  |
| ½ tsp.   | pepper                                |
| 2 Tbsp.  | onion, chopped                        |

Preheat oven to 350°. Combine all ingredients except chicken in a saucepan; simmer ten minutes. This forms your barbecue sauce. Wash and dry chicken and place in a large baking pan. Pour half of the barbecue sauce over chicken and bake uncovered 50–60 minutes, basting with remaining sauce every fifteen minutes.

**Option:** immerse chicken in sauce then remove and cook on a grill, basting frequently.

Serves 4 at only 260 calories per serving.

# Shrimp Scampi

*Linda*

Who says eating
healthy has to
be without flavor
and pizzazz?

| | |
|---|---|
| 4 tsp. | olive oil |
| 1 ¼ lbs. | medium shrimp, peeled (tails left on) and deveined |
| 6–8 cloves | garlic, minced |
| ¾ cup | low-sodium chicken broth |
| ¼ cup | fresh lemon juice |
| ¼ cup | parsley, minced |
| ¼ tsp. | salt |
| ¼ tsp. | freshly ground pepper |
| 4 | lemon slices |

Sauté the shrimp for 2–3 minutes in olive oil or until shrimp is just pink. Add garlic and stir for about 30 seconds. Transfer shrimp to platter and keep hot.

In the skillet, combine the broth, lemon juice, parsley, salt, and pepper and bring to a boil. Boil, uncovered, until the sauce is reduced by half. Spoon sauce over the shrimp. Serve garnished with the lemon slices.

Serves 4.

This low-calorie recipe will help you keep what my daddy used to call my "schoolgirl figure."

# Lemon Baked Fish

| | |
|---|---|
| 1 ½ lbs. | whitefish |
| 3 tsp. | margarine |
| 1 tsp. | grated lemon rind |
| 4 tsp. | lemon juice |
| ¼ tsp. | dried basil |
| | salt and pepper, to taste |

Preheat oven to 400°. Place fish in an ovenproof dish. Blend together remaining ingredients and pour over fish. Cover with foil and bake for 20–25 minutes or until fish flakes easily when tested with a fork. To make lower-sodium, cut salt or use a salt substitute.

Serves 4.

# Oriental Skillet

| | |
|---|---|
| 4 Tbsp. | soy sauce, divided |
| 3 Tbsp. | water |
| 1 lb. | chicken breasts, cut into strips |
| 1 cup | onion, chopped |
| 1 cup | rice, uncooked |
| 1 (10½ oz.) can | chicken broth |
| 1 can | water |
| ½ | green pepper, chopped |
| ½ cup | water chestnuts, chopped |

Spray large or electric skillet with nonstick vegetable oil spray. Add 1 tablespoon soy sauce and 3 tablespoons of water and turn heat to high. Sear meat. Stir in onion, rice, broth, 3 tablespoons soy sauce, and 1 can water. Bring to boil. Reduce heat, cover, and simmer for 25 minutes. Stir in green pepper and water chestnuts. Heat 5–7 more minutes and serve.

*Linda*

I love to use my electric skillet for these kinds of dishes. Substitute chicken with 1 pound of beef strips for variety.

# Lemon Barbecued Chicken

This low-cal, low-salt recipe is wonderful for those times when my husband and I are trying to lose a pound or more.

|  | |
|---|---|
| 6 | chicken breasts |
| 1 tsp. | lemon rind, grated |
| 1 ½ tsp. | salt (or salt substitute) |
| ½ tsp. | dry mustard |
| ½ tsp. | dried oregano leaves |
| 1 tsp. | Worcestershire sauce |
| ½ cup | lemon juice |
| ½ cup | salad oil |
| 2 Tbsp. | scallions, chopped |

Mix lemon rind, salt, dry mustard, oregano, and Worcestershire sauce in small bowl. Gradually stir in lemon juice, then oil and scallions. Pour over chicken in large bowl; marinate in refrigerator for 2 hours. Remove chicken from marinade and place skin side down on grill. Set 3–6 inches from charcoal that has reached light gray stage. Cook for 45 minutes to 1 hour, turning once.

Note: marinade imparts a very good flavor and drains from the chicken so that no more than 5 grams of oil remains on each piece.

Serves 6.

# Linda's Low-Fat Twice-Baked Potatoes

|       |                          |
|------:|--------------------------|
| 6     | large baking potatoes    |
| ½ cup | or more cottage cheese   |
|       | garlic and salt, to taste |
| 4     | green onions, minced     |
| 1 cup | low-fat cheese           |
|       | paprika                  |

Wrap potatoes in foil then bake at 425° for 60 minutes or until done. Cut a slice from top of potatoes and scoop out the pulp. In blender, whip potato, garlic, salt, and cottage cheese until fluffy. Stir in green onions. Spoon the mixture back into the foil-wrapped shells, mounding potatoes slightly. Place the stuffed potatoes on a baking sheet and sprinkle with low-fat cheese. Dust with paprika. Return potatoes to oven until lightly brown.

**Linda**

I love to eat this for lunch with a green salad, though it's great to serve as a side dish for any family meal. This dish has it all, flavor and protein, plus it's low in calories and fat.

Even desserts and snacks can be lower in calories and high in flavor at the same time. This recipe is only 212 calories per serving (for 2 cookies) and less than 1 gram of fat per serving.

# Low-Fat Banana Oatmeal Cookies

| | |
|---|---|
| ½ cup | brown sugar |
| 1 cup | fat free margarine |
| 1 tsp. | vanilla extract |
| 2 | egg whites |
| 2 cups | flour |
| 1 tsp. | baking soda |
| ⅛ tsp. | salt |
| 1 tsp. | ground cloves |
| 1 tsp. | cinnamon |
| 3 | ripe bananas, mashed |
| 2 cups | rolled oats |
| 1 cup | miniature semisweet chocolate chips |

Preheat oven to 375°. In a large bowl cream sugar, margarine, vanilla, and egg whites. Combine flour, baking soda, salt, cloves, and cinnamon. Stir into the creamed mixture. Add the mashed bananas, rolled oats, and chocolate chips; mix until well blended.

Drop dough by using a rounded teaspoon about 2 inches apart on an ungreased cookie sheet. (You can also use an air bake cookie sheet with parchment paper.) You can make the cookies larger, but don't forget the fat grams will increase per cookie. Bake 8 to 10 minutes or until golden brown.

# Chicken Salad

|         |                              |
|---------|------------------------------|
| 1 cup   | chicken (cooked and chopped) |
| ¼ cup   | celery, diced                |
| ¼ cup   | green pepper, diced          |
| ½ cup   | green peas, cooked           |
| 2       | stuffed olives, chopped fine |
| 4       | lettuce leaves               |
|         | salt and pepper, to taste    |
| 8 Tbsp. | low-fat mayonnaise           |

Place all ingredients, except lettuce, in a large bowl and stir. Serve chicken mixture on lettuce leaves.

Serves 4.

## Linda

Make a lovely batch of chicken salad, pull out the crackers, garnish your plate with fresh fruit. All you have left to do is call your best friend to join you for lunch.

Perfect for a
summer picnic
or outdoor
barbecue and
only 44 calories
per serving.

## Low-Calorie Strawberry Chiffon Dessert

| | |
|---|---|
| 1 (4 serving) envelope | low-calorie strawberry gelatin |
| 1 cup | boiling water |
| 1 pint | strawberries, hulled and crushed |
| 1 Tbsp. | lemon juice |
| 1 cup | low-calorie whipped topping |

Dissolve gelatin in boiling water. Stir in strawberries and lemon juice. Chill until slightly thickened. Fold in whipped topping. Spoon into individual dessert dishes. Chill until set, about 2 hours.

Serves 6.

## Low-Calorie Italian Baked Chicken

| | |
|---:|---|
| 4–5 | boneless chicken breasts |
| 1 (4 oz.) can | sliced mushrooms |
| 1 cup | canned tomato sauce |
| 1 Tbsp. | onion, minced |
| ¼ tsp. | garlic powder |
| 1 tsp. | oregano |
| 1 tsp. | basil |
| | nonstick vegetable oil spray |

Preheat oven to 350°. Spray baking pan with vegetable oil. Place chicken breasts in pan. Spread the mushrooms over the chicken. To make sauce, combine tomato sauce, onion, garlic, oregano, and basil in bowl then spread over chicken. Bake uncovered for 45 minutes.
   Serves 4–5.

*Linda*

Here's a quick and delicious low-calorie meal that will be a hit with the girlfriends, or even your family.

# The Frozen Chosen

The only things I inherited from my Grandmother Evans, who departed to heaven when I was only five, were her hand-stitched Sunbonnet Sue quilt and her favorite pie recipes. What treasures!

When I was a young married gal, I decided to make Grandmother's pineapple pie to bring to our church potluck. I followed Grandmother's directions perfectly and plopped the pie into the oven. Later, when I checked on it, I saw it was beautifully browned though it seemed a bit too gooey. I pulled the pie from the oven and placed it on my counter to cool, sure it would set.

I was wrong. An hour later, the pie was still too runny to serve. That's when my freezer saved the day. I tucked the pie inside my freezer's frozen depths. In the next couple of hours, my pie turned from a runny pineapple pudding in a crust to a semi-frozen pineapple custard.

Arriving late to the picnic, I hid my frozen pie between the other desserts and watched to see if the pie would melt before my friends had a chance to sample it.

When my fellow potluckers heard about the frozen pie, they hurried to grab a slice. Not only did my pie help them beat the heat, it was the hit of the afternoon.

Today, when my grandmother's pie is still in the oven, I check it by inserting a toothpick into its heart. When the toothpick comes out clean, I know the pie is ready. I still sometimes serve this pie warm, or even chilled, but I have to admit that it never tasted as good as the day I served it frozen at the church potluck.

Linda

# *Potluck's* Just Desserts

## DESSERTS

You won't have to look too hard to see that this recipe is easy. But that doesn't mean it's not delicious!

# Eva's Chocolate Cream Pie

|        |        |
|--------|--------|
| 4 | egg yolks (reserve 3 egg whites for meringue) |
| 2¼ cups | milk |
| 1 cup | sugar |
| 2 Tbsp. | cocoa (should be heaping) |
| 2 Tbsp. | flour (should be heaping) |
| 2 Tbsp. | butter |
| 1 tsp. | vanilla |
|  | pie shell (baked) |

Beat egg yolks and ¼ cup milk until thick. Add sugar and cocoa and flour. Add remaining milk. Cook over medium heat until thick. Add butter and vanilla. Let cool and pour into baked pie crust.

|        |        |
|--------|--------|
| 3 | egg whites |
|  | pinch of salt |
| ½ cup | sugar |

Place three egg whites in a bowl. Add a pinch of salt. Begin mixing on medium speed and mix until frothy (don't mix too fast or for too long). Begin to add sugar to mixture, slowly, and continue adding and mixing until egg whites become whiter, thicker, and begin to show signs of peaking. Stop mixer, take a little of the mixture out with a spatula, and test with your finger. If the mixture peaks, it's ready. Top pie and bake, 400° for about 5 mnutes. (Be sure to watch the pie. When the peaks brown, it's done.)

# Grandmother's Coconut Chess Pie

|          |                          |
|----------|--------------------------|
| 2        | eggs                     |
| 1 Tbsp.  | flour (should be heaping)|
| ⅛ tsp.   | salt                     |
| ¼ cup    | white sugar              |
| ¾ cup    | white Karo syrup         |
| 1 tsp.   | vanilla                  |
|          | unbaked pie shell        |
| ¼ lb.    | butter                   |
| 12–14 oz.| coconut (can or bag)     |

Beat eggs well and set aside. In mixing bowl blend flour, salt, and sugar, then add eggs. Next add syrup and vanilla, beat until well mixed. Pour mixture into unbaked pie shell. Slice butter into thick slices and cover top of pie. Sprinkle coconut on top of pie and bake for about 1 hour at 300° or until firm and brown.

Serves 8.

*Linda*

I inherited this recipe from my Grandmother Evans. It's one of the best pies I've ever tasted!

About twice a year I'll throw a dinner party. Here's a traditional dessert for just the right touch to the end of the meal.

# Individual Baked Alaska

| | |
|---|---|
| 1 package | sponge shortcakes (four) |
| 1 pint | vanilla ice cream |
| 1 (7.2 oz.) package | fluffy white frosting mix |

Cover baking sheet with aluminum foil. Arrange shortcakes on foil. Place scoop of ice cream in each shortcake. Freeze at least one hour. (Note: shortcakes can stay frozen up to 24 hours at this point.)

Heat oven to 500°. Prepare frosting as directed on package. Completely cover shortcake and ice cream with frosting, sealing it to foil on baking sheet. Bake on lowest rack in oven 3 to 5 minutes or until frosting is light brown. Serve immediately.

Serves 4.

# Laura's Microwave Mint Fudge

|  |  |
|---|---|
| 1½ sticks | margarine |
| 3 cups | sugar |
| 1 small can | evaporated milk |
| ¼ tsp. | salt |
| 1 tsp. | peppermint extract |
| 1½ cups | chocolate chips |
| 1 (7 oz.) jar | marshmallow cream |

Melt margarine in the microwave for one minute. Add sugar, evaporated milk, and salt and mix together. Cook in microwave for 6 minutes then stir boiling mixture, cook for 3 more minutes, and stir, then cook an additional 3 minutes and stir.

Then, stir in peppermint, chocolate chips, and marshmallow cream until blended. Pour into buttered 9-by-13 pan.

*Linda*

With my daughter in a wheelchair, we look for creative ways to "bake" without going to the kitchen. Here's something we make in the microwave in her room.

This takes a little work and you'll need a food processor, but it's worth it.

# Strawberry Pie

| | |
|---|---|
| 1 cup | flour |
| ¼ tsp. | salt |
| 6 Tbsp. | butter |
| 1 | egg yolk |
| 2 Tbsp. | ice cold water |

Add flour, salt, and butter to the bowl of a food processor. Process for several seconds. Add the egg yolk and water. Process just until dough forms. Shape the dough into a ball and wrap in plastic and refrigerate for 1–2 hours. Preheat oven to 425°. Roll out pastry to an 11-inch circle. Line pastry neatly into 9-inch tart or pie pan. Bake for 12 minutes or until golden brown.

| | |
|---|---|
| 1½ quarts | fresh strawberries |
| 1 cup | granulated sugar |
| 3 Tbsp. | cornstarch |
| ¼ tsp. | salt |
| 1 Tbsp. | lemon juice |
| ⅔ cup | fresh orange juice |

In a saucepan over medium heat, combine the granulated sugar, cornstarch, salt, lemon juice, and orange juice. Bring to a boil, stirring constantly. Reduce heat to low and cook until it has thickened, approximately 10 minutes total cooking time. Let the glaze cool.

**Preparation of the Berries**

Wash and hull strawberries. Dry completely. Arrange the strawberries in the baked pie shell, placing the pointed ends up. Brush the orange glaze over the strawberries to cover them completely. Refrigerate.

**When Ready to Serve**

          1 cup   whipping cream
                    confectioners' sugar

When ready to serve, whip the cream and sweeten with a little confectioners' sugar. Cut the pie into wedges and serve with the whipped cream.

Here's a no-bake,
easy-to-make
panful of yum!

# Chocolate Éclair Dessert

### Ingredients for Bottom Layer

| | |
|---|---|
| 2 (3 ¾ oz.) packages | French vanilla pudding |
| 3 cups | milk |
| 8 oz. | Cool Whip |
| | package of graham crackers |

### Ingredients for Fudge Syrup

| | |
|---|---|
| 1 stick | margarine |
| ¼ cup | milk |
| ⅓ cup | cocoa |
| 1 cup | sugar |
| 1 tsp. | vanilla |

Place one layer of graham crackers in bottom of 9-by-13 pan.

Next, mix powdered pudding mixes with 3 cups milk. Fold in Cool Whip. Layer over graham crackers. Keep cool in refrigerator until ready for fudge syrup.

To make syrup, melt margarine in a saucepan till boiling. Add milk, cocoa, and sugar and boil again for one minute. Remove from heat, cool slightly, and add vanilla. When cool to the touch, pour over pudding and graham cracker layers. Refrigerate until serving.

# Eva's Lemon Meringue Pie

| | |
|---|---|
| 1 | large lemon |
| ¾ cup | sugar |
| 2 Tbsp. | cornstarch |
| 1 Tbsp. | all-purpose flour |
| 3 | large eggs, separated |
| 1 ¼ cups | water |
| ¼ stick | butter |
| | pie shell (baked) |

Begin process by grating rind of lemon. Then squeeze lemon so that its juice is added. Mix the juice and rind with sugar, cornstarch, and flour. Add well-beaten egg yolks, water, and butter. Cook in double boiler until it thickens, stirring constantly. Then cool. Once cool, add to prepared pie shell.

## Ingredients for Meringue

| | |
|---|---|
| 3 | egg whites |
| | pinch of salt |
| 3 Tbsp. | sugar |
| 1 tsp. | vanilla |

## Directions for Meringue

Beat egg whites with long strokes until foamy and add a pinch of salt. Beat 25 strokes. Then add 1 Tbsp. sugar. Beat 50 strokes then add another Tbsp. sugar, then 50 strokes, then 1 Tbsp. sugar, then 50 strokes. Add vanilla. Beat until meringue stands in peaks. Top pie filling and bake in a slow oven, 250° for 20 minutes.

*Eva Marie*

What could be better at a summer's picnic than a refreshing lemon meringue pie?

If one could taste heaven, it might taste like this!

# Four Layer Delight

### Ingredients for First Layer

½ cup    butter

⅓ cup    sugar

1 cup    flour

½ cup    pecans, chopped

### Ingredients for Second Layer

1 (8 oz.) package    cream cheese

1 cup    confectioners' sugar

1 (9 oz.) container    Cool Whip

### Ingredients for Third Layer

2 (3¾ oz.) packages instant pudding, any flavor

3 cups    milk

2 tsp.    vanilla flavoring

¼ cup    sugar

### Ingredients for Fourth Layer

remainder Cool Whip

Cream butter, sugar, and flour; add pecans. Pat into 9-by-13 pan. Bake at 350° for 20 minutes. Let cool.

Beat cream cheese and sugar then stir in 2 cups whipped topping. Spread on first layer. Let cool.

Mix instant pudding with milk; add vanilla and sugar. Blend on low speed of electric mixer. Spread on other layers.

Spread whipped topping over pudding. Chill until ready to serve.

# Evans Blackberry Cobbler

| | |
|---|---|
| 3 cups | sugar |
| ½ cup | flour |
| | pinch of salt |
| 1 cup | boiling water |
| 8 cups | fruit (if you don't have blackberries, try other berries. See the frozen section of your grocery store if berries are not in season.) |
| ½ stick | butter |
| ½ tsp. | cinnamon |

In a saucepan, mix together sugar, flour, and salt. Stir in 1 cup boiling water. Boil mixture for one minute as you stir. Next, add 8 cups of fruit. Pour mixture into a 9-by-13 pan. Dot top of cobbler with butter then sprinkle with cinnamon. Bake at 400° for 30–40 minutes.

*Linda*

My dad and I always picked pails of ripe dewberries (which can be substituted for blackberries) every summer. The worst mistake I ever made was coaxing my younger brother into trying this cobbler, hot from the oven and topped with a scoop of melting vanilla ice cream. After that, he was my main competition for this wonderful dessert!

You don't see a lot of egg custard served anymore. It's an old favorite that should never go out of style. My grandmother used to make some of the best!

# Old-fashioned Egg Custard

| | |
|---|---|
| 1 | unbaked 9-inch pastry shell |
| 4 | eggs |
| 2¼ cups | milk |
| ⅔ cup | sugar |
| 1 tsp. | vanilla |
| ¼ tsp. | salt |
| | nutmeg (optional) |

Preheat oven to 400°. Bake prepared pastry shell for 5 minutes (do not prick). Cool on wire rack. Beat eggs in a mixing bowl. Add milk, sugar, vanilla, and salt; blend well. Pour filling into pastry shell; sprinkle with nutmeg as desired. Bake for 15 minutes. Reduce oven temperature to 325°. Bake for 35 to 40 minutes or until knife inserted one inch from center comes out clean. Do not overbake. Cool on wire rack.

# Verna's Peach Cobbler

| | |
|---:|:---|
| 6 cups | sliced peaches |
| 2 Tbsp. | cornstarch |
| 1½ cups | sugar |
| ½ tsp. | almond extract |
| ½ cup | butter or margarine |
| 2 | pie crusts |
| ¼ tsp. | nutmeg |
| 1 tsp. | sugar |

Place peaches in large cooking pot. Mix cornstarch with sugar and stir into peaches. Simmer over medium heat until slightly thick. Stir in almond extract and butter.

Roll out one pie crust and cover sides and bottom of a 9-by-13 baking pan. Pour in hot peach mixture. Roll out second pie crust and cut into thin 1 inch strips. Lay strips over pie in a crisscross pattern. Mix ¼ tsp. nutmeg with 1 tsp. sugar and sprinkle over top crust. Bake in preheated 400° oven for 30–40 minutes.

*Linda*

Try my mom's fresh peach cobbler hot from the oven with a scoop of ice cream. Need I say more?

# Key Lime Pie

*Eva Marie*

Key lime pie is a staple here in Florida. If you've never eaten it, try it on a warm or hot evening and you'll understand why it's so popular.

|            |                   |
|-----------:|-------------------|
| 6          | egg yolks         |
| ½ cup      | lime juice        |
| 1 (15 oz.) can | condensed milk |
|            | pie shell (baked) |

Combine egg yolks, lime juice, and condensed milk. Beat thoroughly and let stand for a few minutes. Pour into pie shell and refrigerate. Top with whipped cream.

# Linda's Graham Cracker Toffee Sticks

| | |
|---|---|
| 1 cup | margarine |
| 1 cup | brown sugar |
| 1 box | graham crackers |
| 1 package | milk chocolate chips |
| ½ cup | walnuts or pecans, finely chopped |

Bring margarine to a boil and add brown sugar.

Grease (or spray) two large 10-by-15 baking sheets with ¾ inch rims. Break graham crackers into 1-by-2 inch rectangles and spread over cookie sheets. Pour ½ boiling syrup over each pan of graham crackers. Bake at 350° for 5 minutes, using top rack only. Sprinkle milk chocolate chips and chopped nuts over top. Let cool.

Linda

You would think this little recipe wouldn't be such a treasure. Enjoy!

# Blueberry Nut Crunch

Another end-of-the-meal hit at dinner parties.

| | |
|---|---|
| 1 (20 oz.) can | crushed pineapple |
| 3 cups | fresh or frozen blueberries (fresh, as always, is best) |
| ¾ cup | sugar |
| ¼ lb. | butter or margarine, melted (butter is better and has just as many calories) |
| 1 box | yellow cake mix |
| 1 cup | pecans, chopped |

Preheat oven to 350°. Lightly grease a 9-by-13 baking dish and spread the undrained pineapple over the bottom of the pan. Add the layer of blueberries and ½ cup of sugar. Drizzle part of the melted butter over the fruit layers, then sprinkle the box of cake mix on top. Drizzle remaining melted butter all over the layer of dry cake mix; top it with a generous amount of pecans. Finally, for a crunch glaze, sprinkle the remaining ¼ cup sugar on top. Bake for about 35–40 minutes or until cake mix is done.

**Note:** after the cake has cooked for about 25 minutes, take a spoon and cut down through the cake to the bottom of the pan. Do this in many places to permit juice to come up.

You can serve with whipped topping if you prefer.

# Oreo Cookies and Pudding Delight

| | |
|---:|:---|
| 1 small package | Oreos |
| 8 oz. | cream cheese, softened |
| 3¼ cups | milk |
| 1 cup | confectioners' sugar |
| 4–6 cups | Lite Cool Whip |
| 2 (3¾ oz.) packages | pistachio instant pudding mix |

Crumble 1 small package Oreos in food processor or crush with rolling pin. Sprinkle three-quarters of the crushed Oreos in bottom of 9-by-13 covered dish. Next, beat softened cream cheese in mixer with ¼ cup milk. Beat in 1 cup confectioners' sugar. Add 1 to 2 cups Cool Whip. Should be soft but not runny. Spoon over crushed Oreos.

Mix packages of pistachio instant pudding with remaining 3 cups milk according to directions on pudding package. Add 1 cup Cool Whip. Spread over cream cheese mixture.

Spread about 2 cups Cool Whip over pudding then sprinkle remaining crushed Oreos over top of Cool Whip. Chill until ready to serve.

*Linda*

Serve this no-bake refreshing treat for a summer's night dessert!

# Southern Ambrosia

A Southern delicacy that has always graced my mother's holiday table. It's called the food of the gods in Greek mythology because eating it made them immortal.

| | |
|---|---|
| 1 (8 oz.) container | frozen whipped topping, thawed |
| 2 ½ cups | coconut, shredded |
| ½ cup | walnuts, chopped |
| 1 (8 oz.) can | fruit cocktail, drained |
| 1 (8 oz.) can | pineapple chunks, drained |
| 1 (11 oz.) can | mandarin oranges, drained |
| 3 cups | miniature marshmallows |
| 1 (10 oz.) jar | maraschino cherries, drained (optional) |
| 1 tsp. | nutmeg |
| 1 tsp. | cinnamon |

In a large bowl, combine the whipped topping, coconut, chopped nuts, fruit cocktail, pineapple, mandarin oranges, marshmallows, cherries, nutmeg, and cinnamon. Mix together well and refrigerate for 30–45 minutes.

## Grandmother Evans's Pineapple Pie

*Linda*

| | |
|---:|:---|
| 2 | eggs |
| ¼ cup | butter |
| 3 Tbsp. | flour (for high altitude baking, add an extra Tbsp. flour) |
| 1½ cups | sugar |
| ½ cup | pineapple juice |
| ½ cup | milk (or cream) |
| ⅔ cup | pineapple |
| 1 | pie shell (unbaked) |

Beat eggs, add butter. Mix flour and sugar; add to egg mixture. Add pineapple juice. Add milk, then pineapple. Mix and pour into unbaked pie shell. Bake at 350° for 50–60 minutes or until the pie is set. This pie can be baked ahead of time, then frozen to be warmed and served at a later date.

Let's just say that because this is one of my all-time favorite pies, I've eaten way past my share. Now it's your turn.

# Chocolate Fudge

*Eva Marie*

Call it a dessert or call it an afternoon treat with a cup of coffee, any time is the right time for homemade fudge.

| | |
|---|---|
| ½ stick | butter |
| 3 Tbsp. | cocoa |
| 3 cups | sugar |
| 1 small can | evaporated milk |
| ½ cup | Karo syrup |
| ½ tsp. | salt |
| 1 cup | nuts |
| 1 tsp. | vanilla |

Melt butter over low heat. Add cocoa and stir. Add sugar, milk, syrup, and salt and mix well. Cook slowly until soft. Let cool. Add nuts and vanilla. Beat until heavy and mixture holds its shape. Pour into 8-inch square buttered dish. Cut into squares.

## Eva's Georgia Pumpkin Pie

| | |
|---:|---|
| 2 | eggs |
| 1 cup | sugar |
| 1 heaping Tbsp. | flour |
| 1 tsp. | cinnamon |
| ½ tsp. | salt |
| ¼ tsp. | ginger |
| ¼ tsp. | allspice |
| 1 cup | pumpkin |
| 1 cup | milk |
| 1 | unbaked pie shell |

Preheat oven to 350°. Beat eggs with beater. Add all dry ingredients, then beat again. Add pumpkin and beat. Add milk. Pour into unbaked pie shell. Bake 1 hour.

*Eva Marie*

Just thinking of this reminds me of Thanksgiving back home and all the wonderful scents that go with the holiday.

# Potluck Characters

When I attend Potluck Book Club potluck gatherings as the guest author, I am often asked how Linda and I created such "yummy" characters. True-to-life, would-know-these-women-anywhere kind of characters. Here's the story.

Linda and I went to the beach one day, and while sitting under a large umbrella and watching the tide roll in, we created six individual, unforgettable women . . . the kind of ladies we know, the ones we've met at church socials, at the women's retreats where we speak, or even within our own families. We might have even added a tad of our own personalities! Each of us writes three of the characters.

Evangeline was the first character I came up with, and one of the characters I write. Like me, she's not a "fan" of the kitchen because she fancies herself as not being able to cook very well. In reality, she's a fine cook; she's just not crazy about the time it takes. Evie—as we call her—would rather be doing something else . . . like running the lives of others.

The next character I created was Lizzie. Lizzie the librarian. Or, in our more modern terms, the "media specialist." I thought of a friend of mine as I drew Lizzie's character blueprint. She is a high school media specialist; she's level-headed and walks on a firm foundation of faith. Lizzie is a good cook but doesn't always have a lot of time because of her work and family. So for Lizzie, quick, easy, and delicious are the names of the game.

Then I created Goldie. Goldie, like me, grew up in Georgia. Like me, she knows all the Southern ways of cooking, of living, and of loving. In the opening chapters of the first Potluck book (*The Potluck Club*), Goldie's life is veiled in both tragedy and the old "if I don't call it what it is, maybe it will go away" mentality. Yet, since she is Southern, the strength of her ancestors rose up in her and declared independence from heartbreak.

In many ways I feel as if these women are as real as my friends, my daughters, my female family members—and the joy in attending potluck functions where the books are being discussed is that readers feel the same way too.

Eva Marie

# *Potluck* Munches Brunch

## BREAKFAST

Easy egg and cheese dish—layer and bake!

# Egg Strata

| | |
|---|---|
| 16 oz. | cottage cheese |
| ¾ stick | butter, melted |
| 6 oz. | Velveeta Cheese |
| 2 oz. | sharp cheese |
| 2 Tbsp. | flour |
| 4 | eggs, beaten |

Grease 2-quart flat baking pan. Place ingredients into layers as listed. Bake in 350° oven for 45 minutes. Makes a sort of soufflé.
   Serves 8.

## Eva's French Toast Soufflé

*Eva Marie*

A simple way to impress your overnight guests!

|           |                                      |
|-----------|--------------------------------------|
|           | bread cubes (½ to ¾ inch square)     |
| ½ cup     | butter, softened                     |
| 8 oz.     | cream cheese, softened               |
| ½ cup     | maple syrup                          |
| 12        | large eggs                           |
| 3 cups    | half and half                        |
| 1 ½ tsp.  | vanilla                              |
|           | cinnamon                             |

Butter 12 ramekins or two 7-by-11 baking dishes well. Fill dishes half full with bread cubes. In small bowl, mix butter, cream cheese, and syrup together after softening in microwave. (It's okay to leave a little lumpy.) Spoon this mixture over bread cubes and distribute evenly clear to edges.

In large bowl, beat eggs, half and half, and vanilla. Pour over bread. Your bread cubes will be "floating" at this point—make sure all cubes are moistened. Dust with cinnamon, cover, and store overnight in refrigerator.

Bake in a 350° oven for 55–60 minutes. It is done when center is raised and firm and whole top is lightly browned. To serve, cut in serving pieces (we cut 6 per casserole dish). Top with diced strawberries and/or sliced bananas and chopped walnuts, then pour on small amount of maple syrup and dust with powdered sugar. Serve immediately; it crashes quickly.

Serves 12.

# Yoder's Old-fashioned Oatmeal Cake

*Linda*

Once when I was speaking behind Yoder's Grocery store in Lancaster, Pennsylvania, I was treated to oatmeal cake for breakfast. I'd never tried this wheatless cake before and fell in love with its chewy texture. Now I make this treat for my family.

| | |
|---|---|
| 1 cup | old-fashioned oatmeal |
| 1 ¼ cups | boiling water |
| ½ cup | vegetable shortening |
| 1 cup | sugar |
| 1 cup | light brown sugar, packed |
| 2 | large eggs |
| 1 ½ cups | all-purpose flour |
| 1 tsp. | baking soda |
| ½ tsp. | salt |
| 1 tsp. | cinnamon |
| 1 tsp. | nutmeg |

Mix oats and boiling water in mixing bowl. Let oats thicken for 20 minutes. Heat oven to 350° then combine shortening, white and brown sugar, and eggs in large mixing bowl. Beat well with mixer, then fold in oatmeal.

In a separate bowl sift flour, baking soda, salt, cinnamon, and nutmeg. Add to oatmeal mixture. Blend well and pour batter into greased and floured 9-by-13 baking pan. Bake for 30 minutes or until cake pulls away from sides or toothpick or knife inserted into the center of cake comes out clean. Serve warm with maple syrup or honey.

# Denver Omelet

| | |
|---|---|
| 2 Tbsp. | butter |
| 1 cup | onion, chopped |
| ½ cup | red bell pepper, chopped |
| ½ cup | green bell pepper, chopped |
| ½ cup | cooked ham, diced |
| 8 slices | cooked bacon, drained and crumbled |
| 4 | large eggs |
| ½ tsp. | salt |
| ½ tsp. | pepper |
| | a few drops of your favorite hot sauce (optional) |

Melt butter in a large skillet or on a griddle.

Sauté onion, bell pepper, ham, and bacon in the butter until the onion starts to become opaque.

In a small bowl, whip the eggs lightly. Add salt and pepper and hot sauce if desired.

Slowly, stir the eggs into mixture in skillet. Lightly brown on one side. Turn over and lightly brown other side.

Serves 2.

*Eva Marie*

When I first heard of this omelet, I wondered what made it a "Denver" omelet. Whatever the answer, doesn't this look yummy?

The nice thing about this dish is you can prepare it the night before and bake it in the morning.

# Linda's Quick Breakfast Casserole

| 5 slices | bread |
|---|---|
| 1 lb. | ground sausage |
| 1 cup | grated cheese |
| 6 | eggs |
| 2 cups | milk |
| 1 tsp. | salt |
| | dash of pepper |
| 1 can | mushroom soup |

Preheat oven to 350°. Tear 5 slices of bread into pieces and place into bottom of a greased 9-by-13 baking dish. Brown and drain sausage. Spoon sausage over bread and sprinkle with cheese. Beat eggs and add milk, salt, pepper, and undiluted can of mushroom soup. Stir. Pour over the mixture in baking dish. Cover with foil and bake for 45 minutes.

Serves 6–8.

# Crispy Potato Quiche

*Eva Marie*

Easy. Delicious. Good morning, world!

| | |
|---|---|
| 1 (24 oz.) package | frozen shredded hash browns, thawed |
| ⅓ cup | butter, melted |
| 1 cup | shredded hot pepper cheese |
| 1 cup | shredded Swiss cheese |
| 1 cup | diced cooked ham |
| ½ cup | half and half |
| 2 | eggs |
| ¼ tsp. | seasoned salt |

Press thawed hash browns between paper towels to remove moisture. Fit hash browns into greased 10-inch pie plate, forming a solid crust. Brush crust with melted butter, making certain to brush top edges.

Bake at 425° for 25 minutes. Remove from oven. Sprinkle cheeses and ham evenly over bottom of crust. Beat half and half with eggs and seasoned salt. Pour over cheeses and ham.

Bake uncovered at 350° for 30–40 minutes or until knife inserted in center comes out clean.

Serves 6.

## Paul's Breakfast Burritos

Linda

Having trouble getting your family to eat breakfast? My hubby eats a breakfast burrito almost every morning.

1 lb.   ground breakfast sausage

8   eggs

shredded cheese

4   large flour (or 6 medium whole wheat) tortillas

avocado, sliced

salsa

sour cream

Brown sausage in skillet and drain off fat. Scramble eggs in a bowl with a fork and pour eggs into skillet with sausage. Cook on medium heat, stirring until fluffy. Sprinkle with cheese.

Place flour tortillas on paper towel and microwave until warm. Fill each tortilla with egg/sausage mixture and top with sliced avocado, salsa, and sour cream. Serve hot.

Serves 4.

# Peach Streusel Coffee Cake

### Streusel

| | |
|---|---|
| ½ cup | Quaker Oats (uncooked, quick or old fashioned) |
| ⅓ cup | sugar |
| 3 Tbsp. | butter, melted |
| ½ tsp. | ground cinnamon |
| ⅛ tsp. | ground nutmeg |

Combine all ingredients for streusel in bowl and set aside.

### Coffee Cake

| | |
|---|---|
| 1 cup | sugar |
| ½ cup | (1 stick) butter, softened |
| 1½ tsp. | vanilla |
| 4 | egg whites |
| 1½ cup | all-purpose flour |
| ¾ cup | Quaker Oats (uncooked, quick or old fashioned) |
| 1 Tbsp. | baking powder |
| ½ tsp. | baking soda |
| ¾ cup | light sour cream |
| 1 (16 oz.) can | sliced peaches |

Beat sugar, butter and vanilla. Add egg whites and mix until smooth. In separate bowl stir together the dry ingredients including the flour, oats, baking powder, and baking soda. Slowly pour dry ingredients into to the egg mixture. Next, fold sour cream into batter and beat until well blended. Pour batter into greased pan.

Drain peaches and blot dry with a paper towel. Arrange peaches on batter then sprinkle batter with the streusel. Bake coffee cake 50 to 55 minutes or until wooden pick inserted in center comes out clean. Serve warm. 16 servings.

*Linda*

You can substitute the canned peaches for a cup of fresh peaches. Based on my personal experience, this recipe disappears the quickest when served warm.

# Meeting Lisa Leann Lambert

A lot of the novels I've read through the years were missing a wonderful ingredient, namely mouthwatering dishes described in full flavor. That's one reason why I've always loved the Mitford series. I licked my lips every time Ester Bolick made one of her famous orange marmalade cakes. How disappointed I was when I flipped to the back of the novels to discover there was no recipe listed for this delight. I felt so close to Ester that I longed to try her recipe myself.

So one of the first decisions Eva and I made while sitting on that Florida beach dreaming up our Potluck series was that food and recipes would tempt our readers throughout the pages of our books. That way our books would have an added dimension, one the readers could taste themselves.

There have been many wonderful food moments in our two Potluck series. For example, who can forget when my character, newcomer Lisa Leann Lambert, cooked her way into the tight Potluck Club circle by offering Evie a warm, delectable cinnamon roll right in the church parking lot? When Evie bit into the gooey roll, what could she say when Lisa Leann announced she was the Potluck Club's newest member? As poor Evie's mouth was full of yum, all she could do was nod in agreement.

Lisa Leann understands the power of food and has wielded that power over others often, first in her many church groups and clubs in Houston, Texas, and now in Summit View, Colorado.

One dish that contributed to Lisa Leann's rise to power was her beef brisket, slathered in barbecue sauce and simmered all night in a hot oven. You'll find that powerful recipe in *The Potluck Club*, but you'll also find that same kind of power in my pecan crusted baked chicken recipe. Try it, and like Lisa Leann, you'll be sure to impress anyone fortunate enough to land an invitation to your table.

Linda

# Potluck Meets Meats

## MEAT DISHES

# Russian Chicken

Linda

If you need an easy-to-prepare dish that will serve 8–12 people, try this. My mom often makes this dish when I visit Mississippi.

| 8–12 | boneless, skinless chicken breast halves, cut in half for smaller servings (or use chicken tenders) |
| 1 can | whole berry cranberry sauce |
| 1 package | Lipton onion soup mix |
| ½ to 1 bottle | Russian salad dressing |
| | cooked long grain and wild rice mix |

Spray 9-by-13 dish with nonstick vegetable oil spray. Layer half of the chicken breasts in baking dish. Mix cranberry sauce, onion soup mix, and Russian salad dressing. Spread half of mix over chicken. Repeat for second layer. Bake covered in 300° oven for 1 hour. Remove cover and bake additional 15 minutes. Serve over cooked long grain and wild rice.

# Pasta Pizza Pie

| | |
|---|---|
| 1 Tbsp. | vegetable oil |
| 1 | large onion, chopped |
| 1 cup | mushrooms, sliced |
| | vegetable cooking spray |
| 1 | egg, beaten |
| ¼ cup | milk |
| 3½ cups | cooked plain corkscrew-shaped pasta |
| 1 cup | shredded part-skim mozzarella cheese |
| 1½ cups | Prego Traditional Italian Sauce or Prego Tomato, Basil, and Garlic Italian Sauce |

Preheat oven to 350°. Heat oil in large skillet over medium heat. Add onion and mushrooms and cook until tender and almost all liquid is evaporated. Remove from heat. Spray 12-inch pizza pan with cooking spray.

Next, mix egg, milk, pasta, and ½ cup of the cheese. Spread pasta mixture in an even layer on prepared pan.

Bake for 20 minutes.

Spread pasta sauce over pasta crust. Top with onion mixture. Sprinkle with remaining cheese. Bake for 18 minutes or until cheese is melted and sauce is hot. Let stand 5 minutes before serving.

Serves 4.

*Eva Marie*

This takes only minutes to prepare and less than an hour to bake. Right up my alley!

# Texas Pepper Steak

Linda

Sharpen your knife
and get ready
to chop. Trust
me; this recipe is
worth the effort.

|          |                                |
|----------|--------------------------------|
| 2 lbs.   | round steak, cut in thin strips |
| ¼ cup    | olive oil                      |
| 1 clove  | garlic                         |
| 1 tsp.   | seasoned salt                  |
| 1–2 Tbsp.| soy sauce                      |
| 1 cup    | water                          |
| 1 cup    | green peppers, cut in strips   |
| 1 cup    | onion, chopped                 |
| ½ cup    | celery, chopped                |
| 1–2 Tbsp.| cornstarch                     |
| 1–2 cups | water                          |
| 2        | medium tomatoes, cut in eighths |
| 2–3 cups | cooked rice                    |

Brown steak strips in olive oil. Add garlic, seasoned salt, soy sauce, and water. Cover and simmer 45 minutes.

Add green peppers, onion, and celery and simmer 10 minutes (covered). Then add cornstarch and 1–2 cups water and cook until thick. If you want more gravy, increase water to two cups.

Add 2 medium tomatoes and simmer 2–3 minutes and serve over hot rice.

# Wild Mushroom Chicken Balsamico

| | |
|---|---|
| 3 tsp. | olive oil or vegetable oil |
| 4 | skinless, boneless chicken breasts (about 1 lb.) |
| 12 oz. (about 3 cups) | assorted wild mushrooms (portobello, shiitake, oyster, or crimini), sliced |
| 1 | medium zucchini, sliced (about 1 ½ cups) |
| 1 | medium onion, cut into wedges |
| 2 cloves | garlic, minced |
| 2 cups | Prego marinara sauce |
| ¼ cup | balsamic vinegar |
| | freshly ground black pepper |

Heat 1 tsp. oil in large nonstick skillet over medium-high heat. Add chicken and cook 10 minutes or until browned. Remove chicken.

Heat remaining oil over medium heat. Add mushrooms, zucchini, and onion and cook until tender. Add garlic and cook 1 minute.

Add pasta sauce and vinegar. Heat to a boil. Return chicken to skillet. Cover and cook over low heat 10 minutes or until chicken is no longer pink. Serve with black pepper.

Serves 4.

*Eva Marie*

Here's a little bit of trivia about me: I absolutely love wild mushrooms! What a delicious way to eat them.

**Linda**

I've made this chili on so many winter nights it's become a Shepherd family classic. Serve with crackers and love.

# Shepherds' Big Batch Chili

| | |
|---:|---|
| 4 lbs. | ground chuck |
| 2 | medium onions, chopped |
| 1 | green pepper, chopped |
| 2 cloves | garlic, minced |
| 3 (14 oz.) cans | diced tomatoes, undrained |
| 4 (8 oz.) cans | tomato sauce |
| 1 (6 oz.) can | tomato paste |
| ¼ cup | chili powder |
| 1 Tbsp. | sugar |
| 1 tsp. | salt |
| 1 tsp. | black pepper |
| ½ tsp. | paprika |
| ½ tsp. | ground red pepper |
| 1 | bay leaf |
| 2 (16 oz.) cans | light red kidney beans |

Brown meat in large skillet until no longer pink. Drain off grease. Add next thirteen ingredients. Cook in Crock-Pot on high for 5–6 hours. Add beans and cook 30 more minutes and serve. Can be served over rice.

# Mushroom Beef Burgers

| | |
|---|---|
| 1 lb. | lean ground round |
| 2 cloves | garlic, minced |
| ½ cup | mushrooms, finely chopped |
| 2 tsp. | Worcestershire sauce |
| ¼ tsp. | freshly ground pepper |
| 4 | whole wheat hamburger buns |
| 1 | small tomato, thinly sliced |
| | spinach leaves |

In a medium bowl, combine ground round, garlic, mushrooms, Worcestershire sauce, and pepper. Shape meat mixture into 4 patties. Cover and chill 1 hour.

Coat grill rack (indoor or outdoor) with nonstick cooking spray. Preheat grill to medium-high heat. Grill burgers, covered, four to six minutes or until a meat thermometer registers 160°.

Serve on buns with tomato and spinach.

Serves 4.

**Option:** if you choose to broil indoors, coat rack of broiling pan with nonstick cooking spray. Set oven shelf about 5½ inches from broiler. Place burgers on rack; preheat broiler. With oven door partially open, broil burgers 3–5 minutes on each side.

*Eva Marie*

Great for an outdoor cookout but designed for indoor cooking.

# Pigs-in-a-Blanket

This is always a big hit with the kids and great at parties too.

little smoky sausages

crescent rolls or canned biscuits

Boil pot of water and remove from heat. Add sausages and let sit 5–10 minutes. Drain.

Cut the crescent roll triangles into two triangles. Wrap a triangle around a sausage. Put bottom of triangle flat on baking pan. (If using biscuit dough, divide dough into ten pieces and patty-cake each piece of dough between your hands until dough pieces are semi-flat, then wrap dough around sausages. Place dough-wrapped sausages in bottom of baking pan.) Bake pan of wrapped sausages at 350° for 8–10 minutes. Serve.

**Note:** these wrapped sausages can be frozen. After you defrost them, bake at 350° until warm.

# Forgotten Chicken and Rice

| | |
|---|---|
| 1 (10½ oz.) can | cream of celery soup |
| 2 cups | milk |
| 1 cup | dry rice (not quick or instant rice) |
| 1 envelope | dry onion soup mix |
| 1 | whole fryer (cut up) or your favorite chicken parts |
| | salt and pepper, to taste |

Preheat oven to 325°. Mix celery soup, milk, rice, and onion soup mix together. Pour into an 11-by-7 baking dish. Lay lightly salted and peppered chicken in rice mixture. Cover and bake for two hours. Serves 4.

*Eva Marie*

I don't know about the rest of the country, but chicken and rice is a Southern favorite.

Cook this to
impress the crowd.

# Linda's Pecan Crusted Baked Chicken

| 3 lbs. | boneless chicken breasts (halves or tenders) |
| 3 Tbsp. | olive oil |
| 2 Tbsp. | lemon juice |
| 1 cup | crushed crackers |
| ⅓ cup | pecans, finely chopped |
| 2 Tbsp. | parmesan cheese |
| 1 Tbsp. | seasoned salt |

Thaw chicken pieces. Mix olive oil and lemon juice. Mix cracker crumbs with chopped pecans, cheese, and seasoned salt. Dip chicken in olive oil mixture and roll in cracker crumb mixture. Place foil on bottom of cookie sheets and spray with Pam or cooking spray. Place open cooling racks on top of foil. Place chicken pieces on racks so chicken will stay crisp as it bakes. Bake at 350° for approximately 45 minutes to 1 hour.

# Greek Style Mahimahi

| | |
|---|---|
| 1 ¼ lbs. | mahimahi fillets, ¾ to 1 inch thick |
| ½ cup | lemon juice |
| ⅓ cup | olive oil |
| 3 Tbsp. | fresh oregano, chopped |
| 3 Tbsp. | fresh mint, chopped |
| 1 tsp. | bottled minced garlic |
| 1 tsp. | lemon peel, finely grated |
| ¼ tsp. | salt |

Rinse fish, pat dry with paper towels. Cut fish into 4 serving-size pieces. Place fish in a resealable plastic bag. Stir together lemon juice, olive oil, oregano, mint, garlic, lemon peel, and salt. Pour over fish; seal bag. Turn to coat fish; marinate in refrigerator for one half hour.

Drain fish, reserving marinade. Coat grilling rack with nonstick cooking spray; preheat grill to medium heat. Grill fish, turning once and brushing with marinade halfway through, 8–12 minutes or until fish flakes easily with fork. Discard remaining marinade.

Serves 4.

*Eva Marie*

I was introduced to mahimahi a few years ago and have loved it ever since. This recipe makes a wonderful dish of a seafood favorite.

Here's a family favorite recipe that's two variations for the price of one. Try both!

# Mom's Chicken or Spicy Shrimp Casserole

| | |
|---|---|
| 2 lbs. | shrimp or 5–6 chicken breasts |
| 1 cup | onion, chopped |
| 1–3 stalks | celery, chopped |
| 1 cup | bell pepper, chopped |
| 2 Tbsp. | butter |
| 3 cups | cooked rice (do not use instant) |
| 1 can | cream of mushroom soup |
| 1 can | cream of chicken soup |
| 1 cup | green onions, chopped |
| 1 small jar | pimento |
| 1 to 1 ½ cups | grated Cheddar cheese |
| | salt, to taste |
| | pepper, to taste |

Boil shrimp (or chicken breasts) until tender. When cool, drain shrimp (or chicken) and save 1 ½ cups broth.

Sauté onions, celery, and bell pepper in butter. Mix with 3 cups cooked rice. Add soup and 1–2 cups shrimp broth (or chicken broth), green onions, and pimento. Add chopped shrimp (or chicken). Season to taste. Sprinkle with cheese. Bake at 375°, 20–25 minutes until bubbly.

**Note:** this dish can be mixed in advance and refrigerated overnight.

# Salisbury Steak

| | |
|---|---|
| 1 lb. | ground beef |
| ⅓ cup | onion, finely chopped |
| ¼ cup | saltine cracker crumbs |
| 1 | egg white, slightly beaten |
| 2 Tbsp. | milk |
| 1 Tbsp. | prepared horseradish |
| ¼ tsp. | salt |
| ⅛ tsp. | pepper |
| 1 (12 oz.) jar | mushroom gravy |

In a medium bowl, combine ground beef, onion, cracker crumbs, egg white, milk, horseradish, salt, and pepper, mixing lightly but thoroughly. Shape into 4 oval half-inch thick patties.

Heat large nonstick skillet over medium heat until hot. Place beef patties in skillet; cook 7–8 minutes or until no longer pink, turning once. Remove from skillet; keep warm.

Add gravy to skillet; heat through. Pour over steak and serve. Serves 4.

*Eva Marie*

Wonderful served with mashed potatoes and sweet English peas.

# Eva's Favorite Scene

Another question I am often asked—and I know Linda is too—is "What was your favorite scene?"

Of course, the answer changes book to book.

In *The Potluck Club* (book one), my favorite scene to write—the one that made me laugh the hardest, I'll have to say—was when the ladies were driving Leigh to the hospital to have her baby. The one I got the most wrapped up in, however, was when Donna and Evie got into verbal fisticuffs in the middle of downtown Summit View, our fictional town located in the mountains of Colorado. There was a lot of tension, a lot of truth revealing, and a lot of "this is what happens when you jump to conclusions" in that scene.

Book three, *Takes the Cake*, had a scene in it that had me laughing so hard I nearly hurt myself. This was when Goldie and Jack are on their way up to the mountains (when an avalanche traps them) and Goldie has set a few "revenge" tactics in place, which, of course, the avalanche does nothing to help and she is now stuck with a man she both loves and despises.

Book two of the Potluck Catering Club series holds my all-time favorite scene from all the books combined. This is when Evangeline and Lisa Leann—who are in New York City together—get separated while on the subway. The trivia of the story is that this actually happened to Linda and me while we were in New York plotting out the book.

But nothing will ever touch me like the scene in *The Secret's in the Sauce* in which Evangeline goes to the single-wide trailer where Doreen, her nemesis and Donna's mother, lives. She confronts her about the hurtful things that happened between the two of them when they were children and asks her about what happened to her after she disappeared from Summit View. It was a "put your feet in my moccasins" kind of moment and a time when I felt my written words were conveying God's plan of forgiveness between his children.

Eva Marie

# *Potluck* Dishes It Up

## CASSEROLES

# Turkey Enchilada Casserole

**Linda**

We always made this dish following the holidays. What a great thing to do with your leftover turkey.

|           |                                              |
|-----------|----------------------------------------------|
| 1 lb.     | ground turkey                                |
| ½ cup     | onion, chopped                               |
| 1 cup     | tomato sauce                                 |
| ½ cup     | water                                        |
| 2 tsp.    | taco seasoning                               |
| 4         | corn tortillas                               |
| 8 oz.     | grated Cheddar cheese (low-calorie or nonfat cheese) |
|           | salt and pepper, to taste                    |

Brown turkey and onion. Add tomato sauce, water, and taco seasoning. Simmer until slightly thickened. In a 1½ quart casserole dish, layer tortilla, ¼ meat, ¼ cheese until gone. Bake at 350° for 25 minutes.

Serves 6–8.

# Harvest Casserole

| | |
|---|---|
| 3 lbs. | hamburger meat |
| 1 | large Vidalia onion, chopped |
| 2 cups | celery, chopped |
| | butter (for cooking celery) |
| 1 (8 oz.) package | egg noodles |
| 1 (13 oz.) can | evaporated milk |
| 3 (10 oz.) cans | cream of mushroom soup |
| ¾ lb. box | Velveeta cheese, grated |

Cook hamburger and onion together. Cook celery in a small amount of butter. Cook noodles as directed on package.

Drain grease from hamburger mixture.

Mix all ingredients together. Place in large casserole dish and bake at 350° until bubbly.

**Option:** rather than using a large casserole dish, use three smaller ones; bake one and freeze the others for another meal.

*Eva Marie*

This recipe calls for an onion from the Georgia town known for its onion harvest: Vidalia (very near my family home). If you cannot find a Vidalia onion, I'm sure any onion will do.

# Linda's Chicken Tortilla Casserole

| | |
|---|---|
| 2 ½ Tbsp. | onion, chopped |
| ¼ cup | butter |
| 3 Tbsp. | flour |
| 1 ½ cups | milk |
| ¾ cup | chicken broth |
| 1 tsp. | salt |
| 3 Tbsp. | jalapeño peppers |
| 1 ½ cups | canned stewed tomatoes, chopped |
| 3 cups | cubed chicken, cooked |
| ½ cup | shredded cheese |
| 12 | tortillas, cut into 1-inch strips |

Sauté onions in butter, then add flour and cook until mixture is bubbly. Stir in milk and broth gradually. Stir in salt, peppers, and tomatoes.

In casserole dish, layer chicken, cheese, then strips of tortillas. Pour sauce over layers then sprinkle casserole with cheese.

Bake at 350° for 30 minutes or until bubbly. Serve hot.

Serves 6–8.

# Sunday-after-Church Pot Roast Casserole

|  | |
|---|---|
| 2 lbs. | boneless beef chuck roast |
| ½ tsp. | salt |
| ¼ tsp. | ground black pepper |
| 1 (8 oz.) bottle | Catalina dressing, divided |
| 2 | large onions, sliced |
| 2 lbs. | Yukon Gold potatoes, peeled and cut into 1-inch pieces (substitute: 2 lbs. red potatoes) |
| 1 lb. | carrots, peeled and cut into 1-inch pieces |
|  | parsley, chopped |
| 2–3 Tbsp. | flour (optional) |

Season both sides of roast with salt and pepper. Brown meat in large heavy pot or Dutch oven on high heat in ¼ cup of the Catalina dressing, turning to brown both sides (very important). Add onions; stir to brown.

Add remaining Catalina dressing, potatoes, carrots, and enough water to come ¾ way up meat (about 1½ to 2 cups). Bring to boil; cover. Reduce heat to low. Simmer 2-plus hours or until meat and vegetables are tender.

(Option: you can brown potatoes with meat if so desired.)

Remove meat from pan; slice meat thinly against the grain. Serve meat and vegetables topped with pan gravy. Sprinkle with chopped parsley just before serving.

If thicker pan gravy is desired, stir ¼ cup water into 2–3 tablespoons flour in small bowl. Remove meat and vegetables from pan; bring liquid to boil on medium-high heat. Gradually whisk flour mixture into pan liquid until thickened to desired consistency.

*Eva Marie*

The key to this recipe is the Catalina dressing. You won't be sorry you tried this.

Easy to make
and perfect for
a quick dish.

# Tuna and Chips Casserole

| | |
|---|---|
| 1 package | macaroni and cheese dinner |
| 1 (7 oz.) can | tuna, drained and flaked |
| 1 can | condensed cream of mushroom soup |
| ½ cup | milk |
| 1 Tbsp. | onion, chopped |
| 1 tsp. | lemon juice |
| 1 cup | potato chips, crushed |

Prepare mac and cheese according to package directions. Add tuna, soup, milk, onion, and lemon juice. Pour into 1½ quart casserole. Top with potato chips and bake at 350° for 20 minutes.
    Serves 6–8.

# Broccoli Casserole

*Eva Marie*

| | |
|---|---|
| 2 (10-oz.) packages | frozen chopped broccoli |
| 1 can | cream of mushroom soup |
| 1 cup | grated Cheddar cheese |
| 2 | eggs |
| 1 cup | mayonnaise |
| 1 cup | crushed Ritz (or Ritz-type) crackers |
| | chopped or shredded leftover turkey (chicken works well too), optional |

Preheat oven to 350°. Cook chopped broccoli until tender; drain.

Add cream of mushroom soup, cheese, eggs, mayonnaise, and turkey (optional). Stir together and place in buttered (option: cooking spray oil) casserole dish. Top with crackers.

Bake for 35–40 minutes.

My mother-in-law found this recipe during the holidays one year and tried it. Since then it has become a favorite for the leftover turkey from our family meals.

Here's a real winner, and the kids love it.

# Taco Casserole

| | |
|---|---|
| 1 lb. | ground beef |
| 2 cups | taco chips, crushed |
| 1 cup | sour cream |
| 1 cup | cottage cheese |
| 2 cups | medium picante sauce |
| ½ cup | onion, diced (optional) |
| 1½ cups | shredded light cheese |
| 1–2 cups | shredded lettuce |
| 1 cup | tomato, chopped |
| 1 (4.25 oz.) can | black olives, chopped |

Preheat oven to 350°. Brown ground beef and drain. In casserole dish, layer taco chips, ground meat, sour cream, cottage cheese, picante sauce, onions, and shredded cheese until the dish is almost full. Cover with foil and bake for 30 minutes or until bubbly. Top with shredded lettuce, chopped tomatoes, and chopped black olives.
Serves 6–8.

# Chicken and Dressing Casserole

*Eva Marie*

My mother shared
this recipe with
me when I was
a young bride.

| | |
|---|---|
| 4 lbs. | chicken |
| 2 tsp. | salt |
| 2 | peeled onions |
| 4 stalks | celery, sliced |
| 1 | carrot, sliced |
| 1 can | cream of chicken soup |
| 1 can | cream of celery soup |
| ¼ cup | cooking sherry |
| 12 oz. | evaporated milk |
| 8 oz. | seasoned breadcrumbs |
| ¼ cup | butter, melted |
| 1 cup | slivered almonds |

Preheat oven to 325°. Cook chicken in a large pot with the salt, onion, celery, and carrot. When done, remove the meat from the bone; tear chicken into small pieces. Purée vegetables in a food processor along with one cup of the chicken stock. In a saucepan, heat soups, sherry, and evaporated milk. Mix with vegetable purée. In a bowl mix breadcrumbs and butter.

Pour one cup of the soup mixture in the bottom of a large casserole dish, topping with one half of the stuffing and then half of the chicken. Repeat and finish by topping with nuts. Bake for 30–40 minutes.

Serves 8.

# Chinese Casserole

Linda

If you're craving
Chinese, here's
a great dish
you'll enjoy.

| | |
|---|---|
| 1 can | mushroom soup |
| ¼ cup | water |
| 1 Tbsp. | soy sauce |
| 2 (7 oz.) cans | solid pack tuna |
| 1 cup | whole cashews |
| 1 (4 oz.) can | button mushrooms, drained |
| ¼ cup | green onions, chopped |
| 1 cup | celery, chopped |
| 2 cups | canned Chinese chow mein noodles |

Mix soup, water, and soy sauce. Drain tuna and flake with a fork. Add to soup mixture. Mix in nuts, mushrooms, onions, and celery. Add noodles, holding back one cup.

Gently mix then spoon into casserole dish, topping with remaining noodles. Bake at 375°, uncovered, for 40 minutes.

Serves 6–8.

# Eva's Chicken Potpie

| | |
|---|---|
| 2 (10¾ oz.) cans | cream of potato soup |
| 1 (16 oz.) can or package | drained mixed vegetables |
| 2 cups | cooked, diced chicken |
| ½ cup | milk |
| ½ tsp. | thyme |
| ½ tsp. | black pepper |
| 2 | pie shells |

Combine first 6 ingredients. Spoon into prepared pie crust. Cover with top crust; crimp edges to seal. Slit top of crust. Bake at 375° for 40 minutes. Cool 10 minutes.

*Eva Marie*

I love this recipe for its simplicity and delicious flavor.

# Layered Writing

Writing a novel with a partner is a lot like creating a layered salad. Each layer is fresh and good alone, but when you stack the ingredients, one on top of the other, you create something completely different: you create a meal.

Writing with Eva is just like that—with each layer (or chapter) one of us creates, the other responds with another fresh insight or adventure.

I recall writing a chapter about my character, Deputy Donna, as she sat outside a local tavern at closing time. She was there in an official capacity, ready to offer tipsy patrons a ride home. That's when she discovered that Goldie's husband was inside this establishment and in the company of (yikes) another woman.

I sent my chapter to Eva and held my breath. What would she do with the revelation that Goldie's husband was cheating on her?

Eva wrote a breathtaking chapter about the pain of a woman betrayed. It's one of my many favorite scenes in *The Potluck Club*.

Another favorite scene of mine resides in *The Potluck Club—Trouble's Brewing*, where Donna tries to rescue a family from a mountain river flood. That initial scene climaxes later in the book in a snowy scene where Donna at last faces a secret of her past as her friends and family reach out to her in love.

The funny thing is, with each new book, I have a new favorite scene, including the scene in *The Secret's in the Sauce* where Donna's detective work arrests a dirty little secret that Lisa Leann has been trying to keep under wraps.

Stay tuned, there are more favorite scenes to come.

Linda

# *Potluck's* Lettuce Cut Up

## SALADS

## Linda's Layer Salad

*Linda*

My mom often made this salad when I was a kid and still makes it for me when I come to visit. It's great for lunch, especially if you top it with canned tuna or salmon. Wait till you see the "secret" ingredient in the dressing.

| | |
|---|---|
| 8 cups | cut-up lettuce |
| ½ cup | sliced celery |
| 1 cup | shredded carrots |
| ½ cup | minced onions |
| ½ cup | cut-up green pepper |
| 1 can | green peas |
| 6 oz. | grated Cheddar cheese |
| ⅓ cup | bacon pieces |
| 1 cup | mayonnaise |
| 1 cup | Cool Whip |
| 2 Tbsp. | sugar |

Layer in 2-quart casserole the lettuce, celery, carrots, onion, green pepper, and peas.

Combine mayonnaise, whipped topping, sugar, then spread over layered vegetables. Top with grated cheese and bacon pieces. Refrigerate 8–24 hours before serving.

# Fried Chicken Salad

| | |
|---:|:---|
| 1 (10 oz.) package | mixed baby greens or your favorite package of salad greens |
| 4 | large fried chicken breasts cut into strips or cubes or 8 fried chicken tenders cut into cubes* |
| 3 | boiled eggs, chopped |
| 3 slices | cooked bacon, crumbled |
| 1½ cups | cherry tomatoes or 2 sliced tomatoes |
| 1 | sliced (or cubed) cucumber |

Wash and drain lettuce well. Pat dry with paper towel if necessary. Combine with other ingredients. Toss and serve with ranch dressing.

Serves 4.

*You can prepare your own or drop by your local deli and pick up some crispy chicken.

*Eva Marie*

My preference is ranch dressing with this salad, but if you prefer another salad dressing it can be substituted.

## English Pea Salad

*Linda*

This salad is easy and good. It's the perfect side dish.

| | |
|---|---|
| 2 cups | English peas, drained |
| 1 cup | celery, diced |
| 1 cup | shredded cheese |
| ¼ cup | sour or dill pickles, chopped |
| ¼ cup | pimiento, diced |
| ½ tsp. | salt |
| | pepper |
| | green pepper, chopped (optional) |
| ¼ to ½ cup (to taste) | mayonnaise or salad dressing |
| | lettuce leaf (optional) |

Drain peas. Add other ingredients. Mix with salad dressing, chill. Serve on lettuce leaf (optional).

# Eva's Mango Salad

| | |
|---|---|
| 3 Tbsp. | orange juice |
| 3 Tbsp. | lime juice (best if from a fresh lime) |
| 2 tsp. | sugar |
| ¼ tsp. | hot chili sauce |
| 2 | mangoes, peeled and cubed |
| 1 | large carrot, grated |
| ¼ cup | red bell pepper, chopped |
| ¼ cup | fresh mint, chopped |

Combine juices, sugar, and hot sauce in a small bowl. Combine mango, carrot, bell pepper, and mint in a separate bowl. Toss with juice until the fruit medley is coated. Refrigerate until ready to serve.

Serves 4.

*Eva Marie*

This salad works well at a summer luncheon or to spice up a dinner meal.

*Linda*

Need something
a little nicer than
a can of cranberry
sauce in a bowl?
This salad has
made my holiday
table shine.

## Cranberry Orange Salad

| | |
|---|---|
| 1 cup | whole cranberry sauce |
| 2 cans | mandarin oranges (drained) |
| 1 cup | mini marshmallows |
| ½ cup | pecans, chopped |

Mix all ingredients together.

# Tuna Fish Salad

| | |
|---:|---|
| 1 small can | albacore tuna, packed in water |
| 2 Tbsp. | celery, diced |
| 1 Tbsp. | red onion, diced |
| 1 tsp. | carrot, grated |
| 1 tsp. | Mrs. Dash |
| | mayonnaise (to your liking) |

Mix all ingredients together. Refrigerate before serving for best results. Serve with whole wheat crackers or club crackers.

*Eva Marie*

For salad scooped and served over lettuce leaves or for sandwiches. Perfect for a social brunch or luncheon.

# Stir and Blend Together

I think it amazes readers and those who invite us to Potluck Book Clubs to speak to hear how Linda and I write the books. Six main first person point-of-view characters and two writers sounds like a recipe for disaster. And yet, it works and we've had a blast doing it.

Four of the six novels were written—mostly—at Linda's getaway cabin in Frisco, Colorado. I fly to Denver in January, Linda meets me at the airport, and then we drive up to this remarkable ski-village-type town, filled with enough memorable characters and settings to fill dozens of books. Because it's January, the whole town is blanketed in snow, which is a real treat for this central Floridian. The air is brisk and the fingerprints of God are everywhere.

Linda and I spend our mornings sipping hot coffee and writing. In the afternoons, we take long walks to town, doing a little window-shopping, chatting with the locals, and then stepping over to Butterhorn's restaurant, where we indulge in lattes and sometimes hotcakes or oatmeal topped with fruits and nuts. While enjoying the cuisine as well as the atmosphere, we plot out a few more scenes and chapters, then—tummies filled—we head back up the hill to the cabin where we work until time for dinner. Sometimes we eat out but most nights we take turns cooking.

I've mentioned the trip to New York. What a time we had! By some wild stroke of genius—or lack thereof—Linda and I decided *not* to take a cab from the airport but instead to take the subway, never thinking in terms of stairs, changing trains, large crowds, and more suitcases than we had hands to carry. Our adventure, of course, landed itself in the book too! So, what readers read is mostly true. The amazing thing for us was finding the "angels" along the way . . . those New Yorkers who kindly offered to help carry bags down the steps or up the steps and onto the sidewalk. Still, we took a cab on our return to JFK.

I've loved writing these books. I've enjoyed digging for recipes. I've spent so much time with Evie, Lizzie, Goldie, Donna, Vonnie, and Lisa Leann that I feel as if they're as much a part of the writing duo of Linda and Eva as we are.

The fun thing is that so many others feel the same way too.

Eva Marie

# *Potluck* in a Stew

## SOUPS AND STEWS

This soup will give you a warm feeling all the way down to your toes.

# Garlic Spinach Soup

| | |
|---:|:---|
| 8 oz. | fresh spinach |
| 8 Tbsp. | butter |
| 2 | large onions, diced |
| 3 cups | chicken stock |
| 4 | medium potatoes, diced |
| 2 cloves | garlic, minced |
| 2 cups | heavy cream (do not substitute milk for cream) |
| 2 | large egg yolks |

Rinse spinach and shred before setting aside. Heat 6 tablespoons butter in a 2-quart soup pot and sauté onion. Add the chicken stock and potatoes. Cook on medium heat for 30 minutes. Add the minced garlic and spinach and simmer for another 10 minutes. Stir in cream but be careful to heat without boiling.

In a small bowl, slowly add ½ cup of the soup to the 2 egg yolks and whisk. Add mixture back into the soup pot, stirring constantly until the soup is thickened. Be careful not to boil. Add salt and pepper to taste. Remove from heat and swirl in remaining butter. Serve immediately.

# Broccoli Soup

| | |
|---|---|
| 2 (8 oz.) packages | cream cheese |
| ½ cup | onion, chopped |
| 2 Tbsp. | butter |
| 1 (10 oz.) bag | chopped broccoli (frozen) |
| 2 | chicken bouillon cubes |
| 1½ cups | boiling water |
| 2 cups | milk |
| 1 tsp. | lemon juice |
| 1 tsp. | salt |
| ¼ tsp. | pepper |

Soften cream cheese at room temperature. Sauté onions in butter and set aside. Cook broccoli until tender and drain. Dissolve bouillon cubes in the boiling water. Add cream cheese to dissolved bouillon; cream together. Add other ingredients including first two and simmer on low heat, stirring to stay smooth.

Serves 6.

*Eva Marie*

A nice addition to a dinner party as the appetizer or served with crackers for lunch.

## Cheddar Soup

Linda

The first cool autumn evening deserves to be celebrated with a bowl of this tasty soup.

| | |
|---|---|
| ½ | onion, chopped |
| ½ cup | butter |
| 4 cups | chicken broth |
| 2 cups | water |
| 4 cups | milk |
| 2 tsp. | Worcestershire sauce |
| 1 (15 oz.) jar | Cheese Whiz |
| 4 cups | mild Cheddar cheese |
| | white flour (for thickening) |

Sauté onion in butter. Stir in broth, water, and milk. Bring mixture to a boil then reduce heat to medium. Add Worcestershire, Cheese Whiz, and Cheddar. Stir until completely melted then add white flour for a thicker soup and sprinkle cheese on top. Serve hot.

Serves 6–12 depending on size of serving.

# French Onion Soup

| | |
|---|---|
| 5–7 cups | yellow onions, thinly sliced |
| 3 Tbsp. | butter |
| 1 Tbsp. | oil |
| 1 tsp. | salt |
| ¼ tsp. | sugar (don't omit this, it helps the onions to brown) |
| 3 Tbsp. | flour |
| 2 quarts | boiling brown stock (canned beef bouillon) |
| | salt and pepper, to taste |
| | rounds of hard-toasted French bread |
| 1–2 cups | grated Swiss or Parmesan cheese |

Cook the onions slowly with the butter and oil in a heavy-bottomed 4-quart covered saucepan for 15 minutes. Uncover, raise heat to moderate, and stir in the salt and sugar. Cook for 30–40 minutes, stirring frequently, until the onions have turned an even, deep, golden brown. Sprinkle the flour and stir for three minutes. Off heat, blend in the boiling liquid. Add seasoning to taste. Simmer partially covered for 30–40 minutes more, skimming occasionally. Add bread and grated cheese to the top before serving.

*Eva Marie*

An old favorite of mine. This recipe takes time but is oh so worth it!

# Pear Soup

*Linda*

Sweet and
refreshing. A fun
alternative to
your standard
bowl of soup.

| | |
|---|---|
| 6 Tbsp. | butter |
| 4 | fresh pears, peeled |
| 1 | large potato |
| 1 | leek |
| 4⅓ cups | pear juice |
| 2 cups | chicken stock |
| | black pepper, to taste |
| | salt, to taste |
| 1 | bay leaf |
| 8 oz. | fresh cream |
| | whipped cream |

In soup pot, melt butter on medium heat. Slice pears, potato, and leek and add to the pot. Cook until fruit and vegetables are soft. Pour mixture into blender and blend into liquid. Return liquid to the pot and add the pear juice, chicken stock, black pepper, salt, and bay leaf.

Add cream just before serving. Top with dollops of whipped cream.

# Creamy Potato Soup

| | |
|---|---|
| 2 Tbsp. | butter or margarine |
| 2 Tbsp. | onion, finely chopped |
| 1½ tsp. | salt |
| ¼ tsp. | celery salt |
| ⅛ tsp. | pepper |
| 3½ cups | milk |
| 1⅓ cups | instant mashed potato buds |
| | paprika |
| | snipped parsley (optional) |

In a medium saucepan, heat butter, onion, salt, celery salt, pepper, and milk to boiling (do not allow to boil). Stir in potato buds (dry). Continue cooking until smooth, stirring constantly. Garnish with paprika and parsley.

Makes 4 servings of 1 cup each.

*Eva Marie*

We rarely have cold days here in Florida, but when we do, this is a nice treat for filling us up and keeping us warm.

The perfect meal for a crowd or maybe even company.

# Linda's Elephant Stew

| | |
|---:|---|
| 1 | elephant |
| 100 lbs. | tomatoes |
| half ton | potatoes |
| 1 wheelbarrow | onions |
| 50 lbs. | salt |
| 10 gallons | vinegar |
| 2 | hares |

Cut one elephant into bite-sized chunks (will take about a month). Boil tomatoes, onions, and salt with other ingredients (except hares) in large outdoor pot. Add elephant chunks over high flames till tender. (This will take about 4 weeks.)

Stir in salt and vinegar. Boil for another 5–7 days.

Serves 3,500.

**Note:** if unexpected company arrives, you may want to add the hares, although not many people like hare in their food.

# Potluck Vegetable Beef Stew

| | |
|---:|:---|
| ¾ lb. | lean stew beef, cooked |
| 3 Tbsp. | vegetable oil |
| 2 | onions, chopped |
| 1 (10 oz.) can | beef broth |
| | salt and pepper, to taste |
| ⅓ cup | sugar |
| 1 Tbsp. | celery seed |
| 1 (46 oz.) can | tomato juice |
| 1 (16 oz.) can | corn (kernel) |
| 1 (16 oz.) can | creamed corn |
| 1 (10 or 20 oz.) bag | frozen lima beans |
| 4 | big potatoes, diced |
| 3 | large carrots, chopped into thin coins |
| 1 Tbsp. | parsley flakes |

*Linda*

Have a potluck stew. Follow the instructions and assign your invitees the ingredients to add to the pot when they arrive. Party while this stew brews.

Assign guests to bring tomato juice, corn, lima beans, potatoes, one onion, carrots, and parsley flakes. You will need beef, one onion, oil, and beef broth to have on hand (ahead of time) to prepare the beef stock.

Before your guests arrive, brown stew beef and sauté 1 onion in 3 tablespoons of oil. Add can of beef broth, cover, bring to boil. Simmer until beef is tender. Add salt and pepper, sugar, and celery seed.

As guests arrive, have them clean, peel, and chop (as needed) their "assignment" to add to the already simmering pot: tomato juice, kernel corn, lima beans, diced potatoes, chopped onion, chopped carrots, and parsley flakes. Stir ingredients and bring pot to a boil then reduce heat and simmer for 1 hour. Add creamed corn, stir, cook for 10 minutes more.

While stew is cooking, lead your guests in conversation or other party fun.

# Characters at a Potluck

Recently, when I was in Fresno, California, for a speaking event, I flew in a day early to enjoy a book club's potluck meeting with a group of ladies who'd just finished reading *The Potluck Club*. What fun to go around the overloaded buffet table and heap my plate with many of the dishes described in the book, including Vonnie's famous molasses cookies, two of which landed on my paper plate along with a large helping of Donna Vesey's chicken marsala.

Upon seeing my characters' favorite dishes, I'll have to admit I looked to see where my literary friends were hiding, sure their smiling faces would pop up in the crowd. But even though the famous ladies of the Potluck Club only exist on the pages of our series, their personalities flavored my time with readers who had come to love the characters as much as I do.

Of course, the ladies of the book club wanted to know which of the characters I'd created for the series. We laughed as I shared the fun I had crafting Lisa Leann Lambert, my naughty Texan, who longs to not only be "in the know" but to be "in control"; sweet Vonnie Westbrook, a retired nurse with a shocking secret that comes to knock on her door; and Donna Vesey, my spunky deputy who breaks the hearts of all the fellows of the fictional town of Summit View, Colorado.

The funny thing about this buffet was that there were no vegetable dishes! Never fear, this chapter is loaded with ideas you'll want to serve yourself (and your friends and family).

Linda

# *Potluck* Veggies Out

## VEGETABLES

# Teacher's Broccoli and Rice

Linda

I picked up this recipe in my tenth grade home economics class and cooked it for my mom, dad, and little brother. It became one of their favorite dishes as it's almost a whole meal unto itself.

|  |  |
|---:|---|
| 1 cup | rice, cooked |
| ¼ to ½ cup | onion, chopped |
| ½ cup | celery, chopped |
| 1 Tbsp. | butter |
| 1 or 2 packages | broccoli, chopped and cooked |
| 1 can | cream of chicken soup |
| 1 small jar | Cheese Whiz |
|  | grated parmesan cheese or paprika |

Press rice into a crust inside large, greased casserole. Sauté onions and celery in butter. Combine with broccoli, soup, and Cheese Whiz. Pour over rice. Sprinkle casserole with cheese or paprika. Bake at 350–375° for 10–20 minutes or until bubbly and lightly browned.

# Baked Acorn Squash with Apples

|          |                     |
|---------:|---------------------|
| 1        | acorn squash        |
| 1 ½ cups | apple, chopped      |
| ½ tsp.   | salt                |
| 2 Tbsp.  | brown sugar         |
|          | nutmeg              |
| 1 Tbsp.  | butter or margarine |

Preheat oven to 350°. Cut squash in half and scoop out seeds. Place halves in a shallow baking dish; fill centers with apple. Pour a little water in the bottom of the dish. Cover and bake for 30 minutes or until partly done. Sprinkle with salt, sugar, nutmeg, and dot with butter (margarine). Bake uncovered about 45 minutes or until the squash is soft.

*Eva Marie*

This dish presented at the table makes you look like a gourmet cook when really it's so easy.

# Oven-Broiled Potato Slices

Linda

Skip the fast-food
fries and try this
healthy alternative.
It's scrumptious!

|  | |
|--:|---|
| 2 | medium potatoes |
| 2 Tbsp. | olive oil |
|  | salt |
|  | paprika |

Preheat broiler. Wash but do not pare potatoes. Cut into ¼-inch slices, dip slices in 2 tablespoons olive oil. Season with salt and paprika. Place in pan under hot broiler and brown potatoes about 7 minutes on each side, or until tender.

# Sweet Potato Soufflé

Eva Marie

This recipe has been passed down and altered slightly for generations in the kitchens of women of my family.

3 cups (4 large mashed)    cooked sweet potato (can substitute with 2–3 quart cans)
½ cup    granulated sugar
½ cup    brown sugar
2    eggs
1 tsp.    vanilla
½ cup    canned milk
½ cup    butter, melted
½ tsp.    cinnamon
½ tsp.    nutmeg

Preheat oven to 350°. Combine all ingredients well. Placed in greased casserole dish. Begin preparations for topping.

### Topping

1 cup    brown sugar
⅓ cup    flour
1 cup    nuts, chopped
⅓ cup    butter (not melted)

Combine, mixing together with fork. Sprinkle on top of soufflé mixture.

Bake half hour.

*Linda*

This is a great open-the-can-and-dump-it-into-a-pot recipe. Well, you do have to brown the meat and fry the bacon, but that's not so hard. Try this for a large family gathering.

# Mary's Settler's Beans

| | |
|---|---|
| 12 oz. | lean bacon |
| 1½–2 lbs. | ground meat |
| 1 lb. can | ranch-style beans |
| 1 lb. can | jalapeño pinto beans |
| 1 lb. can | pinto beans |
| 1 lb. can | pork and beans |
| ½ tsp. | seasoned salt |
| 2 tsp. | chili powder |
| 2 Tbsp. | prepared mustard |
| ½ cup | barbecue sauce |
| ½ cup | ketchup |
| ½ cup | sugar |
| ½ cup | Pace picante sauce |

Fry bacon until crisp, drain and crumble. Brown ground meat. Mix all remaining ingredients in large pan. Use wooden spoon to stir so you don't smash the beans. Put bean mixture in large roaster or two large casserole dishes. Cook covered at 350° for 30 minutes. Then cook uncovered for 30 minutes.

# Marinated Carrots

5 cups   sliced carrots

1   small green pepper, slivered

1   medium onion, slivered

1 can   tomato soup

½ cup   salad oil

1 cup   sugar

¾ cup   vinegar

1 tsp.   prepared mustard

1 tsp.   Worcestershire sauce

1 tsp.   salt and pepper combined

Boil carrots until tender, drain and cool. Combine other ingredients and pour over carrots, green pepper, and onion (raw). Refrigerate 12 hours. Drain and serve. Will keep in refrigerator for 2 weeks.

*Eva Marie*

Who says chilled carrots aren't yummy?

Linda

This is a great side
dish and goes
with everything.

# Sweet 'n' Sour Green Beans

| | |
|---|---|
| 2 strips | turkey bacon |
| 1 | small onion, chopped |
| 2 large cans (14.5–16 oz.) | French-style green beans |
| 2–4 Tbsp. | vinegar |
| 1 Tbsp. | brown sugar |

Cut up and fry bacon, remove from fry pan and save. In same fry pan, with drippings, sauté onion. Add green beans and half the bean liquid in can. Add vinegar and brown sugar, then bring to boil and simmer for 15 minutes. Sprinkle with bacon and serve.

# Golden Potato Bake

½ cup    cornflake crumbs

1 tsp.    salt

4–6    medium potatoes, pared

2 Tbsp.    butter or margarine, melted

Heat oven to 375°. Mix cornflake crumbs and salt. Brush potatoes with butter; coat with crumbs. Arrange in ungreased baking pan (9-by-9). Bake uncovered 1 to 1¼ hours or until potatoes are tender.

Serves 4–6.

*Eva Marie*

A simple addition to any meal, a way to fancy it up, let's say.

My mom made this wonderful, rich dish on special occasions. I still share this dish at potlucks.

# Mom's Asparagus Casserole

| | |
|---|---|
| 1 stick | butter |
| 4 to 6 slices | wheat bread (cut into 4 strips per slice) |
| 2 cans | green asparagus spears, drained |
| 1 can | English peas, drained |
| 1 can | mushroom soup |
| 1 can | sliced water chestnuts, drained |
| 10 oz. | grated cheese |

Melt butter in a 9-by-13 casserole dish. Dip bread slices in butter and set aside. Layer asparagus in casserole dish, add English peas. Mix and spread soup over the vegetables, sprinkle water chestnuts over soup. Place the buttered strips of bread over the mixture. Sprinkle with the grated cheese and bake uncovered in 350° oven for 30 minutes.

Serves 6–8.

# Squash Casserole

|  |  |
|---|---|
| 1 | medium onion, sliced |
| 3 Tbsp. | butter |
| 16 | medium yellow crookneck squash, sliced |
| ¾ cup | sour cream |
| 1½ cups | grated Cheddar cheese |
| 1 tsp. | salt |
| ⅛ tsp. | paprika |
| 2 | egg yolks, beaten |
| 3 Tbsp. | chives, chopped |
| ½ cup | crumbled bacon |
|  | bread crumbs |

Preheat oven to 350°. Sauté onion in butter, add squash. Simmer until tender. Drain and add sour cream, cheese, salt, and paprika, stirring over low heat until cheese melts. Remove from heat. Add beaten egg yolks, chives, and bacon. Cover with bread crumbs. Spoon into greased casserole. Bake 30 minutes.

*Eva Marie*

Another Southern favorite and always on my kitchen table during the holidays.

I think you'll be surprised at how good these beets are with any meal.

## Yummy Pineapple Beets

| | |
|---|---|
| 1 (16 oz.) can | sliced beets |
| 1 (16 oz.) can | pineapple chunks |
| 2 Tbsp. | cornstarch |
| ⅓ cup | sugar |
| 1 Tbsp. | vinegar |
| | salt and pepper, to taste |
| 2 Tbsp. | butter |

Drain beets and pineapple, reserving juices. Pour juices in saucepan then cook over medium heat till boiling.

In separate saucepan add cornstarch, sugar, vinegar, salt, and pepper and stir until mixture is a smooth paste. Stir in a small amount of hot juices and stir constantly until paste is thick. Add beets and pineapple, mixing well. Add butter. Simmer 20 minutes.

Serves 8–10.

# Corn Pudding au Gratin

*Eva Marie*

This recipe
reheats nicely.

| | |
|---|---|
| 1 (15 oz.) can | creamed corn |
| 2 Tbsp. | flour |
| 1 cup | cheese, diced |
| ⅛ tsp. | black pepper |
| 2 Tbsp. | margarine |
| 2 | eggs |
| 1 cup | milk |
| 1 cup | buttered bread crumbs |

Preheat oven to 350°. Combine corn, flour, cheese, and pepper; mix well. Add melted margarine and well-beaten eggs. Warm milk and add to mixture. Pour into 1½ quart casserole pan that has been sprayed with cooking spray. Cook in oven until pudding begins to set, then sprinkle buttered bread crumbs over the top and reduce heat to 325° and bake until firm. If bread crumbs are not sufficiently brown when pudding is firm, turn to broil briefly. Cooking time about 30–40 minutes.

Here's a quick side dish that you can whip together in minutes.

## Linda's Cheese Vegetable Bake

| | |
|---|---|
| 1 (20 oz.) package | frozen mixed vegetables like broccoli and cauliflower |
| 2 cans | cream of celery soup |
| 1 | medium onion, chopped |
| 1 cup | Velveeta cheese, cubed |
| ⅓ cup | mayonnaise |

Mix ingredients together and bake at 350° in a casserole dish for 45 minutes. Try different packages of frozen vegetables and combos.

# Zucchini with Cheese

| | |
|---|---|
| 1 ½ lbs. | zucchini |
| ¼ cup | flour |
| 1 ½ tsp. | salt |
| 1 ½ tsp. | dried oregano |
| ¼ tsp. | pepper |
| ¼ cup | olive or salad oil |
| 2 | medium tomatoes, sliced |
| 1 cup | sour cream |
| ½ cup | grated Parmesan cheese |

Preheat oven to 350°. Lightly grease an 8-by-8 baking dish. Scrub zucchini well. Cut crosswise into ¼ inch slices.

In medium bowl, combine flour with ½ tsp. salt, ½ tsp. oregano, and ⅛ tsp. pepper. Toss zucchini slices in seasoned flour to coat well.

Slowly heat oil in large, heavy skillet. Sauté zucchini until golden brown, about 4 minutes on each side. Drain on paper towel. Cover bottom of dish with zucchini. Top with tomatoes. Combine sour cream, rest of salt, oregano, and pepper. Spread evenly over tomato slices. Sprinkle with cheese. Bake 30–35 minutes.

Serves 6.

*Eva Marie*

I think zucchini is too often overlooked as a summer squash. This recipe will help you decide what to serve for dinner tonight as a side to your entrée.

# Cheesy Tomatoes

*Linda*

Simple, healthy,
and delicious.
What more could
you want?

|  |  |
|---|---|
| 2 | medium tomatoes |
| 1 Tbsp. | green onions or chives, chopped |
| 1 tsp. | parsley, chopped |
| ½ tsp. | salt |
| 1 Tbsp. | grated Parmesan cheese |

Cut tomatoes in half and arrange on broiler pan cut side up. Sprinkle tomatoes with onions/chives, parsley, salt, and parmesan. Broil 3–5 inches from heat for about 5 minutes or until cheese is golden brown. Serve immediately.

Serves 4.

# Twenty-four-Hour Coleslaw

| | |
|---|---|
| 1 | cabbage, finely cut |
| 1 | large onion, finely sliced |
| ⅔ cup | sugar |
| 1 cup | vinegar |
| ½ tsp. | dry mustard |
| 1 tsp. | celery seed |
| 1 Tbsp. | salt |
| 1 cup | salad oil |

Place one half of cabbage in large bowl. Cover with onions; add remaining cabbage. Do not mix. Sprinkle sugar over cabbage. Mix vinegar, mustard, celery seed, and salt in pan, bringing to a boil. Add salad oil, let cool. Pour over cabbage, cover, and chill overnight (or 24 hours if you can). Stir when ready to serve.

*Eva Marie*

What is a hot summer Southern day without a barbecue? And what's a barbecue without coleslaw?

# Metric Conversion Guide

## VOLUME

| U.S. Units | Metric |
|---|---|
| ½ teaspoon | 2 ml |
| 1 teaspoon | 5 ml |
| 1 tablespoon | 20 ml |
| ¼ cup | 60 ml |
| ⅓ cup | 80 ml |
| ½ cup | 125 ml |
| ⅔ cup | 170 ml |
| ¾ cup | 190 ml |
| 1 cup | 250 ml |
| 1 quart | 1 liter |

## LENGTH

| Inches | Centimeters |
|---|---|
| 1 | 2.5 |
| 2 | 5.0 |
| 3 | 7.5 |
| 4 | 10.0 |
| 5 | 12.5 |
| 6 | 15.0 |
| 7 | 17.5 |
| 8 | 20.5 |
| 9 | 23.0 |
| 10 | 25.5 |
| 11 | 28.0 |
| 12 | 30.5 |
| 13 | 33.0 |
| 14 | 35.5 |
| 15 | 38.0 |

## TEMPERATURE

| Fahrenheit | Celsius |
|---|---|
| 250° | 120° |
| 275° | 140° |
| 300° | 150° |
| 325° | 160° |
| 350° | 180° |
| 375° | 190° |
| 400° | 200° |
| 425° | 220° |
| 450° | 230° |
| 475° | 240° |
| 500° | 260° |

## WEIGHT

| U.S. Units | Metric |
|---|---|
| 1 ounce | 30 grams |
| 2 ounces | 60 grams |
| 3 ounces | 90 grams |
| 4 ounces (¼ pound) | 125 grams |
| 8 ounces (½ pound) | 225 grams |
| 16 ounces (1 pound) | 500 grams |

**Note**: The recipes in this cookbook have not been developed or tested using metric measures. When converting recipes to metric, some variations in quality may be noted.

# Meet the Authors

Meet Linda Evans Shepherd and Eva Marie Everson, authors of both the Potluck Club and the Potluck Catering Club series.

### How did the Potluck series get its start?

**Linda:** Once, on a getaway weekend in the mountains with my family, I read a novel on friendship. As we were driving home I told my hubby, "If I were to write a book on women's friendships it would be full of humor and deal with real issues. It would be written by real friends, and it would be called *The Potluck Club*."

The vision was so delicious; I immediately dialed Eva Marie on my cell phone. As my hubby drove around curves and through valleys, I described my idea between dropped calls. "It should have six characters," I said, "that interact. I would be in charge of three and so would you."

**Eva:** Now, I'm in an airport and I'm exhausted. I told her I'd call her back then hung up the phone. When I leaned back and closed my eyes, I thought of all the potluck dinners that were held at my little South Georgia church when I was a child. I could see not only the dishes and the food spread but the dynamics of the women behind it. I just started laughing then picked up the phone and called Linda back and said, "Oh my gosh, Linda, we can do this and this," and boom, we were off and running.

**With the two of you living a couple of thousand miles apart, how do you write together?**

**Linda:** The Internet is a wonderful thing! Though Eva and I are in different states, it's as though we're in adjoining offices as Eva emails, "Get ready! One of your characters just pulled a big one!"

Soon the chapter is sent to my inbox and it's time for the reveal. The next thing you know, I open the document and find myself in Summit View, Colorado, with the Potluck girls, delighted and shocked by what my characters did while they were visiting Eva's characters.

All I can say is that when it's my turn to write, I find Potluck revenge is sweet, because a few days later, Eva will be surprised to find out what happened to her characters (insert manic laughter here). Seriously, Eva and I have as much fun discovering the book as our readers do.

**Do you ever write on location?**

**Linda:** Yes! Sometimes I fly to Florida, where Eva lives, and we've even flown to New York. Though, usually we write together in the Colorado high country.

**Eva:** We basically hole up in a mountain cabin and write like maniacs. There were times when I'd look over at the mountains covered in snow on a clear beautiful day. I'd type a couple of minutes and then look over to watch a literal sheet of snow descend from the mountain and glide toward the cabin. Within seconds, everything is white. You can't even see the mountain anymore. For me it's such a display of God's majesty and power. It's so inspiring. I get that same inspiration if I'm standing on the shoreline at the beach. Yet, it's different. There's something about being up in the high country and in the mountains that's different from being in the city. It's breathtaking, and I don't mean that just because there's no oxygen.

**What are the challenges of being co-authors?**

**Linda:** One reason authors like to write novels is to have control over a world, when of course in real life they have no control. That's why a lot of authors would never consider sharing a plot. So, to make co-writing work, you have to be willing to share. You really have to love, trust, and listen to each other. You have to serve one another. Eva and I have captured how to do that. There have been times when we've had disagreements, but because we love each other and because we want what's best for our book, we've worked through the issues.

**Eva:** Let me tell you a little secret. Linda and I are good friends—very good friends—but we don't always see eye-to-eye and we sometimes struggle. Why? Because we're real! We're human. How did we overcome it? We talked it out and we prayed together. That's really the only way you can. Prayer and love will overcome the obstacles.

**How did you think up your characters?**

**Eva:** We thought up our characters on a beach in Cocoa Beach, Florida, after a Christian book tradeshow in 2002. We took a day off and went to the beach, where we sat and talked. First we chose what our characters' occupations would be. Once we came up with that list, we picked who would get to write which character.

Then we let the characters introduce themselves to us individually and then as a pair. I would start writing and would have absolutely no idea what a character might say to me. I can distinctly remember writing Goldie's story and her history of how she met Jack. That bit of writing literally poured out of my head.

**Linda:** I love to go on a "ride along" with members of the police force. Over the years, I've interviewed my police friends about what it's like to be an officer. So when I was ready to write about Donna, I knew exactly what she was about. Also, Vonnie's character is a nurse. After my daughter's accident, I spent so much time with nurses I began to believe I was one. Okay, not really, but let's say I know so many nurses I think I've earned the right to write about one.

**Are the women of Potluck real?**

**Linda:** To Eva and me, yes!

**Eva:** Linda and I have created a "woman for everyone." With six main characters versus the typical "one," it's easy to find at least one you relate to . . . if not two or three! For those women who like to cook, the recipes are an added bonus too! We have received a lot of email, letters, and face-to-face comments on those!

**How can women use the Potluck Club books to develop friendships within their own women's ministry groups?**

**Eva:** Reading groups, baby! Linda and I have been so blessed to be invited by several book clubs that have used the Potluck books as their book of the month. The clubs have "potluck night," bringing the cooked dishes from the recipes in the back of the books. They really talk about the issues we tackle in the books too.

**Linda:** Sometimes we phone in an appearance to a Potluck book club. For more book club ideas, check out www.PotluckClub.com.

**What makes the Potluck Club a fun read?**

**Linda:** Our characters have flaws and struggles, just like real women. But they use humor and their faith in God to rise above their circumstances. But one of the best things about reading the books is to share them with a friend. Then the payoff is you and your friends will have women you can talk about without being guilty of gossip.

**What message would you like the readers to take from the Potluck series of books?**

**Linda:** We women, we friends, need the Lord.

**Eva:** When Linda and I are writing the Potluck Club books, it is my prayer that our readers will come to understand the importance of friendship, its value within God's plan, how precious prayer is (especially with a friend), and that we are—none of us—not too far from the long arm of the Lord. We are also—all of us—capable of falling short of his glory. And, sometimes, God uses friends and friendship to bring us back or to the fullest knowledge of him we can obtain.

**Linda Evans Shepherd** has been married thirty years to Paul and has two young adult children. Linda also serves as the CEO of Right to the Heart Ministries and is an international speaker and media personality. Currently, she's a popular guest host appearing on *Denver Celebration* (Daystar Television); channel host for *Web TV 4 Women*; host of *Web TV 4 Women's* programs, *Be a Miracle*, and *Cooking Up Wonders*; co-host of *Miracle Quest*, a popular internet radio program; publisher of *Right to the Heart of Women* electronic magazine; founder and CEO of AWSA (Advanced Writers and Speakers Association); and host of the webinar platform *Miracle Lane*, where she conducts live online classes.

Linda is also a bestselling author and has written 30 books, including co-authoring the The Potuck Club and The Potluck Catering Club series. Linda's nonfiction book *Share Jesus Without Fear*, co-written with Bill Fay, will soon be in over 100 languages. Look for Linda's book *When You Don't Know What to Pray* from Revell in the spring of 2010.

To find out the latest on Linda or to book Linda to speak at your event, go to www.VisitLinda.com.

Award-winning author and speaker **Eva Marie Everson** is a Southern gal who's not that crazy about being in the kitchen, unless it's to eat! She has been married to a wonderful man, Dennis, for three decades and is a mother and grandmother to the most amazing children in the world.

Eva's writing career and ministry began in 1999 when a friend asked her what she'd want to do for the Lord, if she could do anything at all. "Write and speak," she said. And so it began.

Since that time, she has written, co-written, contributed to, and edited and compiled a number of works, including the award-winning *Reflections of God's Holy Land; a Personal Journey Through Israel* (which includes her photography among the spectacular photographic works), *The Potluck Club/Potluck Catering Club* series (with Linda Evans Shepherd), *Sex, Lies, and the Media, and Sex, Lies, and High School* (co-written with her amazing daughter Jessica). In 2009 Revell will release the first in a new series of southern fiction novels with Eva Marie titled *Things Left Unspoken*. 2010 will see the release of *This Fine Life*.

Eva Marie is both a graduate of Andersonville Theological Seminary and a mentor with the Jerry B. Jenkins Christian Writers Guild. Eva Marie speaks nationally and internationally about her passion: drawing believers to the heartbeat of God. In 2002 she was named AWSA's first Member of the Year. Also that year she was one of six journalists chosen to visit Israel for a special ten-day press tour. She was forever changed.